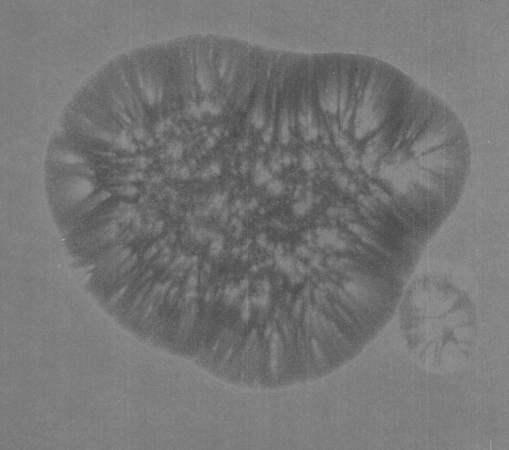

DK Guide to
SAVAGE EARTH

Trevor Day

A Dorling Kindersley Book

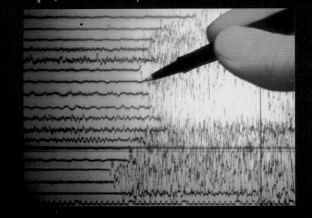

DK

LONDON, NEW YORK, MUNICH, PARIS,
MELBOURNE, DELHI

Project Editor David John
Project Art Editor Elaine Hewson
Editor Lucy Hurst
Senior Editor Fran Jones
Senior Art Editor Marcus James
Category Publisher Jayne Parsons
Managing Art Editor Jacquie Gulliver
DTP Designer Nomazwe Modonko
Picture Research Brenda Clynch
Jacket Design Dean Price
Production Kate Oliver

First published in Great Britain in 2001 by
Dorling Kindersley Limited
80 Strand, London WC2R 0RL

2 4 6 8 10 9 7 5 3

A CIP catalogue record for this book
is available from the British Library

ISBN 0-7513-3075-2

Colour reproduction by GRB Editrice, S.r.l.,Verona

Printed and bound by
Mondadori Printing S.p.A., Verona, Italy

See our complete
catalogue at
www.dk.com

CONTENTS

THE BIG BANG

To understand how our planet was created, we have to look into space. The savage forces that batter, shake, and shape the Earth's surface today were set in motion billions of years ago and are still going strong. Beneath the surface, immense heat causes molten rock to circulate, moving giant sections of the crust, triggering earthquakes, and shooting out molten rock from volcanoes. The enormously high pressures and temperatures deep inside the Earth continue to generate heat through radioactive decay and chemical changes. The Sun, however, has much more power, and without its light and warmth, life here would not exist. But the Earth's story really begins with the biggest explosion the Universe has ever known – the one that created it.

SOMETHING FROM NOTHING

Most scientists now agree that everything we know started with the Big Bang – time, space, and all the matter in the Universe. About 13 billion years ago, the Universe burst into existence with an unimaginably large explosion. The fireball was so concentrated that matter was created spontaneously out of energy. At the instant of creation, the Universe was infinitely hot and dense. Then it expanded and cooled, and created the galaxies, and the stars and planets they contain. About 4.6 billion years ago, our own Solar System came into being.

UNIQUE EARTH

Among the planets in the Solar System, Earth is unique. Seen from space, its swirling clouds and blue oceans show that it has plenty of liquid water. The Earth's gravity is strong enough to trap a protective atmosphere. It is also the right distance from the Sun to have habitable climates. Water and an atmosphere are two conditions vital for the evolution of life as we know it.

STAR MAKER

Inside its whirling clouds of cosmic dust, the spectacular Orion nebula gives birth to stars. Our Sun was created in the same way by the dust of the vast solar nebula, several billion years ago. When the solar nebula grew old, material was drawn into its centre, which became denser and hotter as it generated energy by nuclear fusion. In a gigantic nuclear explosion, the infant Sun was born, and began radiating the first sunshine in our Solar System.

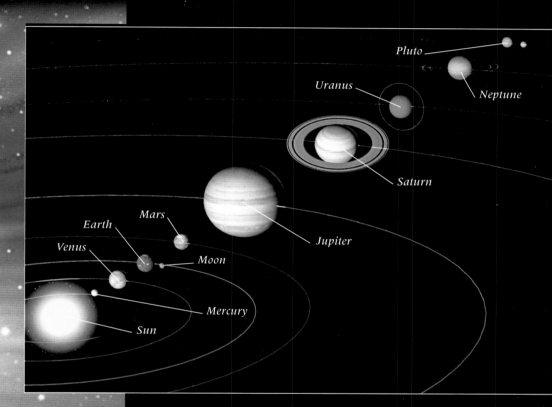

SOLAR SYSTEM

When our Solar System was forming, the early Sun probably lay at the centre of a disc-shaped cloud. Inside the cloud were liquids and gases, swirling around with dust and ice. Under the pull of gravity, dust particles clumped together to form rocks. Metal-rich rocks near the Sun came together to form the inner planets. In the cooler, outer regions, ice combined with rock and lighter gases to form the outer planets.

LIFE ELSEWHERE?

The conditions that allow complex life forms to flourish on Earth might be rare elsewhere in the Universe. Simple microbes, however, can survive in the most hostile places, and may exist on other planets or their moons. In 1996, a Martian meteorite found in Antarctica contained what at first appeared to be fossilized bacteria (*right*). Some scientists believe Mars may once have sustained simple, microbial life.

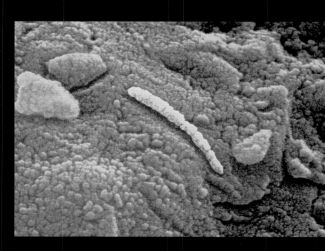

VIOLENT PAST

THE EARLY EARTH WAS A RED-HOT, MOLTEN HELL. Space debris from the collapsed solar nebula was flying in all directions, causing meteorites and comets to smash into the young planet's surface. These violent bombardments raised the Earth's temperature higher and higher. Then, not long after it was formed some 4.6 billion years ago, the Earth was struck by an object the size of Mars. The impact released a heat so intense that it melted the planet. Debris from the impact explosion splashed out into Space and gathered together to form the Moon. But the Earth did not remain searingly hot. It gradually cooled into a planet with a solid surface, oceans, continents, and an atmosphere. In fact, for more than three-quarters of its existence the Earth has sustained living organisms. Now approaching middle-age, the Earth has about five billion years left to bask in the life-giving heat of the Sun.

Atmosphere — Crust

Mantle

Outer core

Molten outer core

Solid inner core

EARTH'S TRANSFORMATION
More than four billion years ago, the Earth's molten rock began to separate into layers. Heavy, iron-rich material sank to the intensely hot core. Silicon and lighter metals floated to the surface to become the crust. Molten rock became sandwiched between the core and crust to form the mantle. On the surface, granite-like rocks thickened the crust and formed the first continents.

BLASTS OF THE PAST
This is an artist's impression of the young Earth's violent landscape. Space debris and lava flows must have ravaged the brittle crust. As meteorites landed, they punched holes in the surface and plunged into the hot interior, sending up huge showers of molten rock. Gradually, the thin surface crust grew thicker. From time to time, slabs of cooled crust plunged back into the molten mantle below and were melted again.

DINO KILLER
For more than 100 million years, the Earth was ruled by dinosaurs. They became extinct quite suddenly about 65 million years ago. Their disappearance was probably caused by a massive meteorite or comet that collided with the Earth. The impact would have shrouded the world in a cloud of dust that blotted out the Sun for many months. In the freezing darkness, most of the world's plant and animal life died, including the dinosaurs. Some small, hibernating racoon-like mammals survived.

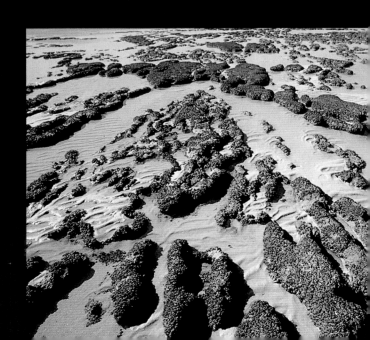

OCEANS

The water that filled the first oceans may have come from comets that collided with the Earth. A comet (*left*) is a giant snowball of ice and rock. Water also came from the steam given off by molten rock (magma) flowing onto the surface. The steam condensed in the atmosphere, formed clouds, and fell to Earth as rain, just as the steam from volcanoes does today.

THE SUN

Our Sun is an average-sized star similar to billions of others in the galaxy. Without its heat, Earth would be uninhabitable. Scientists calculate that the Sun has about five billion years of life left before it uses up its fuel supply of hydrogen. When it does, it will expand 100 times in size into a massive sphere called a red giant, and will destroy the Earth.

ATMOSPHERE

The Earth's early atmosphere was rich in volcano gases such as carbon dioxide. Today's atmosphere has little carbon dioxide, but contains oxygen. The change was caused by early life forms – tiny organisms that released oxygen as waste. These clumps (*left*) are made by microbes called cyanobacteria, which trap sunlight to make food. They are very similar to the early oxygen-making organisms.

ICE AGES

Despite its fiery origins, much of the Earth has been covered in ice during its history. Ice spread from the poles towards the Equator when the climate cooled, and retreated as it warmed. This may have been caused by a slow wobble of the Earth's axis, which alters its distance from the Sun. Present-day glaciers (*left*) show us how the world must have looked during the ice ages.

MOVING CONTINENTS

THE GROUND BENEATH OUR FEET IS NOT AS STEADY as we may think. In fact, the continents that make up most of the Earth's land surface are always on the move, shifted around by forces deep inside the Earth. This movement is known as continental drift. It takes place because the inside of the planet is hot and turbulent. The intense heat generated at the Earth's core is carried upwards where it disturbs the cool, rocky surface. This forces the plates of crust that make up the continents, called tectonic plates, to move. Each year the continents drift by about a centimetre (nearly half an inch). Some are crunching together, some are splitting apart, others are grinding past each other. As this happens the Earth's features are created or changed. Violent earthquakes and volcanoes are dramatic reminders that the plates never stop moving.

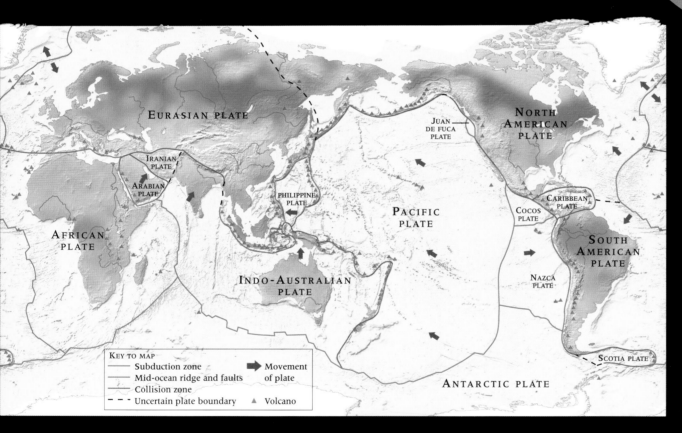

EURASIAN PLATE
IRANIAN PLATE
ARABIAN PLATE
AFRICAN PLATE
PHILIPPINE PLATE
INDO-AUSTRALIAN PLATE
JUAN DE FUCA PLATE
NORTH AMERICAN PLATE
PACIFIC PLATE
COCOS PLATE
CARIBBEAN PLATE
NAZCA PLATE
SOUTH AMERICAN PLATE
SCOTIA PLATE
ANTARCTIC PLATE

KEY TO MAP
— Subduction zone
— Mid-ocean ridge and faults
— Collision zone
‑ ‑ ‑ Uncertain plate boundary
➡ Movement of plate
▲ Volcano

TECTONIC PLATES

Each tectonic plate has a lower layer of solid rock and an upper layer called the crust. The plates float on the Earth's molten, semi-liquid mantle. Where the crust is thin, the Earth's surface is low-lying and covered by seas and oceans. Continents form where the crust is thicker and stands higher. As the tectonic plates move, the continents are carried with them and the oceans change shape.

GLOBAL JIGSAW PUZZLE

The plates that form the Earth's surface fit together like a jigsaw puzzle. This map shows the boundaries of the Earth's plates and the directions in which the plates are drifting. The pieces slowly change shape as they move. Great mountain ranges have formed along the blue zones where plates are colliding. Lines of volcanoes are dotted along the red zones where one plate is sinking (subducting) below another, causing molten rock to erupt to the surface.

THE EVIDENCE

When the German scientist Alfred Wegener stated in 1915 that today's continents were once part of a single landmass, people ridiculed him. But Wegener was right. He argued that although ancient plant fossils, such as the *Glossopteris* fern (*right*) are found on widely separated continents, they could only have come from one original continent. Today, geologists agree with Wegener that the continents did indeed drift apart.

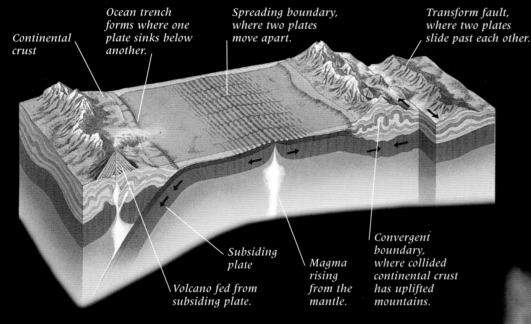

Continental crust

Ocean trench forms where one plate sinks below another.

Spreading boundary, where two plates move apart.

Transform fault, where two plates slide past each other.

Subsiding plate

Volcano fed from subsiding plate.

Magma rising from the mantle.

Convergent boundary, where collided continental crust has uplifted mountains.

PLATE BOUNDARIES

The illustration above shows what happens at the boundaries that separate one plate from another. At spreading boundaries, plates are moving apart, and molten rock (magma) rises up to fill the gaps. Transform faults lie along boundaries where plates scrape past one another, generating earthquakes. Where convergent boundaries are found, plates are pushing together to create mountain ranges in a process of folding and uplifting.

WHEN PLATES COLLIDE

The Andes Mountains of South America extend along the Pacific coast for about 8,900 km (5,530 miles). They began to form about 170 million years ago when the Nazca Plate collided with (and sank beneath) the South American plate. The foothills (*above*) show where a folding, or buckling, of the continental crust has occurred. Mountain-building in the Andes slowed down about 6 million years ago.

WEST OF JAVA

This is Anak Krakatoa in Indonesia, a volcano that first erupted in 1927. It is one of a long string of volcanoes that lies along a boundary where the Indo-Australian plate is sliding below the Eurasian plate. The subsiding plate melts as it is forced downwards into the Earth's mantle, and squeezes magma to the surface to form volcanoes.

SPREADING RIDGES

The Mid-Atlantic Ridge is a spreading plate boundary that stretches from the Arctic to the Southern Ocean. Most of it lies beneath the ocean, but at Thingvellir in Iceland (*left*), it crosses over land. The boundary between the North American plate on the left and the Eurasian plate on the right is clearly visible. Where the plates have moved apart, the crust in between has collapsed, forming a steep-sided rift valley. The region is very active volcanically. In 1963, a huge underwater eruption occurred 130 km (80 miles) south of Thingvellir. Lava rose to fill the gap in the widening ridge, and cooled to form the new island of Surtsey.

VOLCANOES

THERE IS A THUNDEROUS EXPLOSION, the ground trembles, and the sky darkens. A volcano is erupting, firing red-hot boulders into the air and belching out clouds of ash and poisonous fumes. Volcanoes are vents or fissures in the Earth's crust that allow molten rock to rise up from the hot interior and spill onto the surface. An active volcano may erupt continuously, and over time may become a broad mountain with gentle slopes. Other volcanoes may lie dormant (sleeping) for most of the time. They erupt only at rare intervals but with explosions violent enough to destroy their own cones and a wide surrounding area. Many of the Earth's mountains were formerly volcanoes, but are now extinct. Today, there are more than 1,000 active volcanoes on land, and many more under the sea.

INSIDE AN EXPLODING VOLCANO

Beneath the Earth's crust, rock is not the solid stuff we are familiar with, but a very hot, molten liquid called magma. This rises through a gap in the crust and becomes trapped in a magma chamber – a cavity beneath the volcano. As more magma enters, pressure builds up until the volcano's clogged vent is blasted open. The feeder pipe to the vent then acts like a gun barrel that shoots out lava, rocks, ash, and steam.

Cone is built up by successive layers of lava and ash over thousands of years.

Magma collects in the magma chamber and builds up pressure in the clogged vent.

ALL SHAPES AND SIZES

A volcano's shape depends on the thickness of its lava and the frequency and size of its eruptions. Dome volcanoes build up cones from the layers of lava and ash they produce. Fissure volcanoes are fairly flat, and trickle lava from big cracks in the ground. Caldera volcanoes, like this one (*left*) at Crater Lake, Oregon, USA, lie inside vast craters made by a previous, massive explosion that collapsed the original mountain.

HOTSPOT

Most volcanoes occur where the Earth's plates collide or move apart. But some, like the Hawaiian islands, arose in the middle of a plate because they were created by a "hot spot" in the Earth's mantle, which burned through the crust and formed a volcano. The volcano stops erupting as the moving plate carries it away from the hot spot, and a new volcano forms. The chain of islands grows as the plate moves.

Hawaii is formed from the world's tallest volcanic cone. It is a recent island that emerged from the sea within the last million years.

Oahu was created between two and three million years ago by the same hot spot that gave birth to Hawaii.

SLEEPING BEAUTY

The graceful slopes of Mount Fuji in Japan rise more than 3,500 m (12,000 ft) above the surrounding plain. Its perfect cone – built up from layers of lava and ash, is a favourite symbol in Japan. Some believe that gods live in the summit, which is always covered in snow. It last erupted in 1707 and has been dormant ever since.

VOLCANO BREATH

Scientists in Iceland wear gas masks to monitor the poisonous gases escaping from a fumarole – a small volcanic vent. These sites are sampled regularly. An increase of gases, or a change in their mixture, can give an early warning of an eruption.

VOLCANIC WONDERLAND

Over thousands of years, underground water heated by volcanic activity has trickled down the side of this famous plateau at Pamukkale, Turkey. The salts in the water have crystallized to create a magical landscape of "frozen" waterfalls, stalactites, and basins. People have come to bathe in its warm waters since ancient times

ERUPTION!

WHEN A VOLCANO BLOWS ITS TOP, it gets its explosive power from carbon dioxide gas. Immense underground pressures trap the gas in the magma and keep it in a dissolved form. With the sudden release of pressure that occurs when a volcano's vent is unclogged, the gas turns into rapidly expanding bubbles – similar to the burst that happens when you open a shaken bottle of fizzy drink. The bubbles force the magma through the vent in an explosion that throws out fountains of lava, ash, and superheated chunks of rock. Although scientists are getting better at predicting eruptions, they do not know what form an eruption will take. A volcano could produce a gentle lava flow, or a dangerous explosion, and may even change its behaviour mid-eruption.

SPECTACULAR DISPLAY
Mount Stromboli, an island
volcano near Sicily, Italy, is highly
active. Bubbling pools of lava in its 925 m–
(3,040 ft–) high crater produce frequent, small
explosions. People come to watch the yellow-hot
bombs (called pyroclasts) being shot high into the air.
In 1999, a group of tourists camping near the summit
suffered burns and concussions when an unusually intense
explosion bombarded them with lava, rocks, and ash.

MOUNT ST HELENS BLOWS HER TOP

Early on Sunday, 18 May 1980, Mount St Helens, Washington, USA, erupted for the first time in 123 years. Rising pressure inside the volcano made a bulge in its side, causing a landslide of 8,000 million tonnes of rock. The explosion produced a mushroom cloud of gas and ash 19 km (12 miles) high.

FROZEN IN TIME

In AD 79, the people of Pompeii, Italy, were watching Mount Vesuvius erupting. Suddenly, a rolling cloud of scorching ash and gas, called a pyroclastic flow, came sweeping down the mountain towards them. Most died from suffocation before being buried in the ash. Their ghostly figures are revealed by plaster casts made from the cavities their bodies left in the ash.

RED SKY AT NIGHT

Ash from volcanoes can be carried by wind around the world. It blocks and scatters the Sun's rays to produce blood-red sunsets, and cools the Earth. Drifting ash from Mount Pinatubo in the Philippines cooled the Earth's surface during 1991.

PYROCLASTIC POWER

Soon after Mount St Helens' first explosion, a pyroclastic flow rushed down her northern slope at 160 kmh (100 mph). It flattened trees and splintered them to matchwood. Even at the edges of the blast zone, tree trunks were seared, snapped, and stripped of their branches, creating an eerie landscape of devastation.

13

RIVERS OF FIRE

Flowing lava glows, spits, hisses, and crackles, and seems to have a life of its own. Lava is magma that has erupted on to the surface. Hot spot volcanoes, such as Kilauea on Hawaii, produce fiery rivers of bubbly, runny lava. Its surface cools to a thick skin, which breaks as more red-hot lava oozes forwards underneath. This lava poses little danger to people as it rarely flows faster than a walking pace. However, it can travel great distances and is almost impossible to stop. Some explosive volcanoes, such as Mount St Helens, Washington, USA, produce a very thick, pasty lava that looks like ash. It moves at a snail's pace, but can be hundreds of metres deep.

STOPPING THE FLOW
Lava from Mount Etna, Italy (*right*), is flowing towards the town of Zafferana. Although slow moving, lava is very destructive, burning and burying everything in its path. Concrete barriers, trenches, and even explosives are used to divert lava flows away from homes.

LAVA MEETS SEA
Tourists in Hawaii (*left*) are watching the intense glow of hot lava turning sea water into steam. Underwater, the runny lava cools to produce shapes like pillows. Continued eruptions mean the island is always expanding into the sea.

PAHOEHOE FLOW
Two types of lava flow have Hawaiian names. Pahoehoe, shown here, flows from a hot spot vent and develops a skin that wrinkles into rope-like coils. Aa spits or tumbles out of the volcano and cools into crumbly, lumpy shapes.

VOLCANOLOGY

Clad in a heat-reflective suit, this volcanologist can collect samples of hot lava – if he is quick. Volcanoes are very unpredictable. In 1991, husband and wife team Maurice and Katia Krafft were killed by a sudden ash flow on Mount Unzen, Japan. The risks volcanologists take to predict eruptions have saved many lives.

GALAPÁGOS ISLANDS

The Galápagos islands in the Pacific Ocean are still growing. They are fed by lava from a hot spot in the Earth's mantle. Galápagos volcanoes produce lava that flows over wide areas and becomes craggy when cool. Rainfall disappears down its cracks and soil is slow to form, making the islands rugged and relatively barren.

THE LAVA OF LIFE

Volcanic eruptions do not always spell bad news. The land around volcanoes, like these green plains in Mexico, can be made fertile by the occasional shower of ash, which adds nutrients to the soil. But too much ash or lava is a catastrophe for the farmer. Thick lava flows can take months to cool, and decades to weather enough for plants to grow again.

MAKING MOUNTAINS

T HE EARTH'S SPECTACULAR MOUNTAIN RANGES are places of sheer, towering rock, raised up by the movements of tectonic plates. Some mountains are isolated volcanic peaks, built up by successive eruptions. Others are great blocks of rock thrust skywards as the Earth's crust cracks and splits. But most form where one tectonic plate collides with another, causing the crust to buckle and fold. Most of the great mountain ranges of the world, such as the Himalayas in Asia, and the Alps in Europe, were formed in this way, and lie in long chains close to plate boundaries. Mountain ranges have been created and destroyed many times in the Earth's 4.6-billion-year history. As soon as they are lifted up, erosion takes over and wears them away with wind, water, and ice. Mountains that are tall and rugged are usually still growing. Once there is no more uplift, erosion will smooth them down until only gentle hills remain.

Niihau

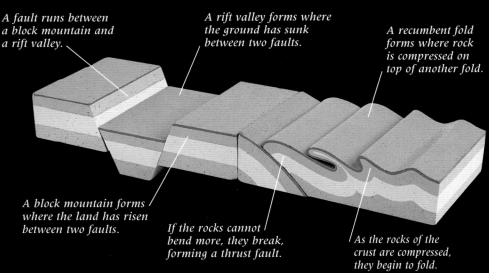

A fault runs between a block mountain and a rift valley.

A rift valley forms where the ground has sunk between two faults.

A recumbent fold forms where rock is compressed on top of another fold.

A block mountain forms where the land has risen between two faults.

If the rocks cannot bend more, they break, forming a thrust fault.

As the rocks of the crust are compressed, they begin to fold.

PUSHING AND SPLITTING
Mountains are formed in three main ways. Fold mountains occur where plate collisions cause the Earth's crust to crumple and fold. Others are created by volcanic eruption. Elsewhere, the crust may fracture to produce cracks called faults. The land alongside the fault may rise or fall, creating block mountains, rift valleys, and cliffs. Moutain-making involves both stretching and compression. This model (*left*) shows the types of folding and fracturing seen in mountain ranges.

YOUNG AND TALL
Mount Everest in the Himalayas, Asia, is the highest point on Earth. In 1999, it was measured accurately at 8,850 m (29,035 ft) above sea level. It may still be rising from a collision that began 50 million years ago, when the Indian tectonic plate collided with Asia. In geological terms, the Himalayas are still very young. Weathering and erosion has sculpted the mountains into their present dramatic shapes, but has not yet begun to wear them down significantly.

Everest's summit is pushed upwards at the rate of 4 mm (0.16 in) a year.

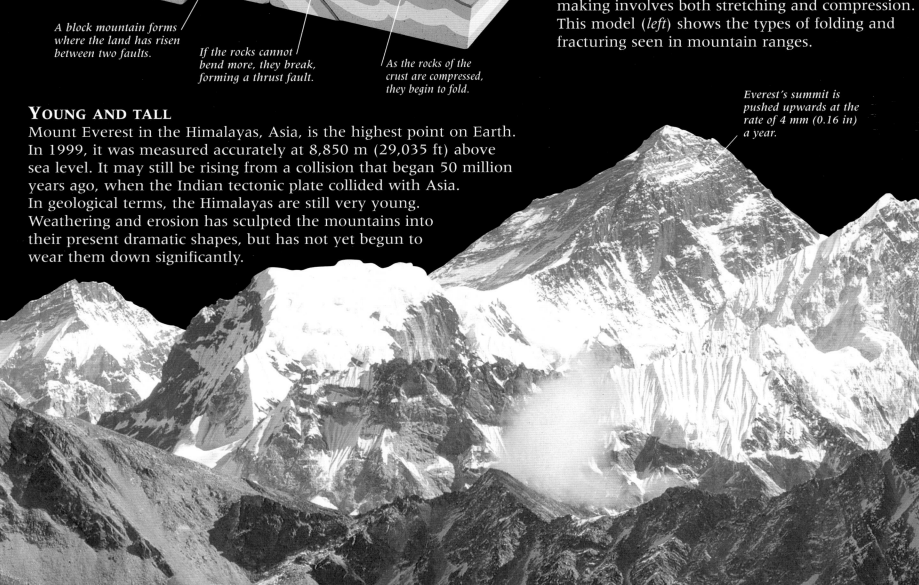

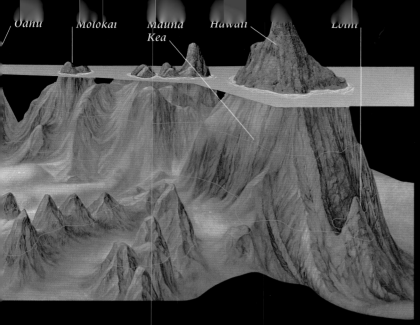

Oahu   Molokai   Mauna   Hawaii   Loihi
                 Kea

Hawaiian giants
Towering above the sea floor are huge submerged mountains. Some are volcanoes that will eventually emerge above the surface. Measured from the sea floor, the volcanic Mauna Kea is really the world's tallest mountain. It rises to a height of 9,632 m (31,601 ft), with its summit on the island of Hawaii. Its volcanic neighbour, Loihi, is still below the water.

Highland erosion
The two landmasses that created Britain were once separated by the ancient Iapetus Ocean. England and Wales lay on one continent and Scotland on another. About 420 million years ago, the two continents collided with a force that slowly formed the Scottish Highlands. Once as high as the Himalayas, the Highlands have been eroded away with only hard granite outcrops, such as Glen Coe (*above*), remaining.

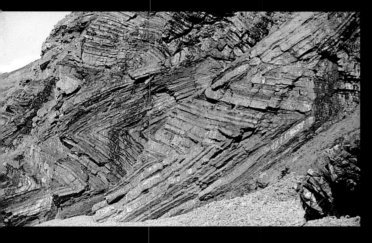

Zig-zag folding
Rocks generally form in flat layers called strata. However solid they may seem to us, rocks stretch, buckle, and fold when squeezed by movements in the Earth's crust. On a large scale, this happens along a mountain range. On a smaller scale, strata sometimes fold into zig-zag patterns, like these shale strata in Cornwall, England, which buckled more than 250 million years ago.

Sir Chris Bonington, who reached Everest's summit at the age of 51, has led several expeditions up Everest's toughest routes.

Extreme environments
The world's highest places can be very hostile to human life. Climbers risk injury from rockslides and avalanches, and may suffer altitude sickness, snow blindness, and frostbite. Technology, such as satellite phones and breathing equipment, helps to improve the safety of climbers.

EARTHQUAKES

FROM A GENTLE SHUDDER to terrifying and violent movements in the Earth, earthquakes literally rock the world. Earthquakes are tremors in the ground, created by the sudden movement of tectonic plates. Most plate boundaries slide past each other, but some get jammed together. The forces pushing the plates then build up until stress causes the rocks to distort. At the moment of rupture, the plates judder past each other and the rocks snap back to their original shapes like springs. This releases a stored energy in the form of seismic waves – the vibrations that cause an earthquake. Most 'quakes are very minor, but others flatten whole cities.

CALIFORNIA'S FAULT

Although tremors can occur anywhere, they are more frequent in earthquake zones. These zones lie near the sliding edges of the tectonic plates, called fault lines. This picture shows the famous San Andreas fault in California. It runs for 1,207 km (750 miles), passing close to the cities of San Francisco and Los Angeles, and causes constant tremors.

TURKISH TREMORS

In August 1999, a devastating earthquake hit the city of Ada Pazari on the western coast of Turkey. More than 3,000 people died when some of the city's poorly built apartment blocks collapsed in the tremor. Survivors are seen here walking on what were once the roofs of their homes. The disaster showed how important it is to build secure structures in earthquake zones.

Inadequately built structures collapsed quickly when the earthquake struck.

Some people survived for a week buried under rubble. Rescuers listened for their tapping sounds.

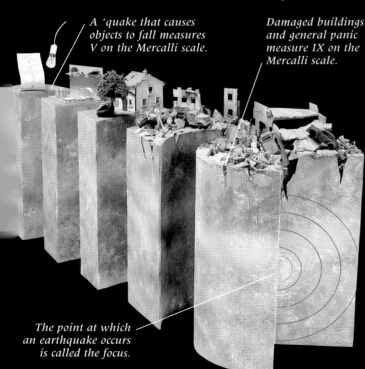

A 'quake that causes objects to fall measures V on the Mercalli scale.

Damaged buildings and general panic measure IX on the Mercalli scale.

The point at which an earthquake occurs is called the focus.

SCALES OF DESTRUCTION

This model shows the effect of an earthquake as it is measured by the Mercalli scale. A swinging lightbulb measures III; total devastation measures XII. The famous Richter scale tells us the strength of an earthquake. It takes readings from a machine called a seismometer, which measures the force of a tremor. The strongest tremor ever recorded measured 8.9, in Chile, in 1960.

RAGING INFERNO

Raging fires are a major hazard after an earthquake strikes. Fires break out when tremors damage electrical equipment and gas pipes. In Kobe, Japan (*right*), fire spread quickly through the city's wooden buildings when firefighters ran out of water. San Francisco was devastated by earthquakes in 1906 and 1991. In both disasters, fire caused huge damage.

Children are taught to duck under desks.

UNSTABLE COUNTRY

Regular safety drills are held in the schools, homes, and workplaces of Japan. Because it lies close to a junction of three tectonic plate margins, Japan experiences hundreds of earthquakes a year. Tremors of various force are recorded every day.

Within seconds, parts of the city were buried beneath tons of rubble.

Many of the city's residents were left homeless by the disaster.

SHOCK WAVES

EARTHQUAKES ARE IMPOSSIBLE TO PREVENT, but they can sometimes be predicted. Scientists use seismographs to detect certain vibrations in the ground called foreshocks. These are minor tremors produced by deep rocks fracturing shortly before an earthquake. In 1975, scientists detected clear foreshocks in China's Haicheng province. Buildings were evacuated before the 'quake struck and few people died. Animals may be sensitive to foreshocks too, and their behaviour can signal approaching earthquakes. Hours before a 'quake flattened Kobe, Japan, in 1995, sealions at the zoo began leaping out of the water and behaving erratically. The main earthquake shock is always followed by smaller ones – aftershocks – caused by the rocks on either side of a fault settling into new positions. Aftershocks cause additional damage and pose a threat to rescuers.

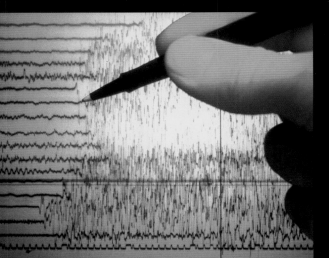

SHOCKING DISPLAY
A scientist points to earthquake shock waves recorded by a modern seismograph. The greater the wave, the wider the zigzagging movement on the seismograph's display. Various horizontal lines across the display record the different frequencies (vibrations) of a shock wave. Seismographs can record the seismic waves from earthquakes thousands of kilometres away.

SHOCK PROOF
The Transamerica Building in San Francisco, USA, is designed to withstand earthquakes. It is built on pads made of rubber and steel and has reinforced concrete walls. These absorb tremors and resist sideways shaking.

THE BIG ONE
On 18 April 1906, massive shock waves along the San Andreas fault destroyed two thirds of San Francisco. The disaster showed that steel-framed buildings, such as the City Hall tower (*above*), were more likely to remain standing and were safer than brick. Today, the city has one of the strictest building codes in the world.

JAPANESE WAVES

When the earthquake struck Kobe, shock waves caused the ground to roll and undulate, like waves in the sea. Soft earth "liquefied" as it moved and the city's raised freeway collapsed, even though it had been strengthened before the 'quake. Destruction like this is caused by surface waves – earthquake vibrations that travel at ground level. Scientists divide surface waves into two types. Love waves move from side to side, and Raleigh waves move up and down, like the sea.

PERSON DETECTOR

When buildings collapse during an earthquake, people are buried alive. Rescuers have a race against time to find survivors. Sensitive equipment, such as this trapped person detector, is used to listen for noises. It can distinguish between background noise and human movement, and can even pick out a human heartbeat.

CHINESE DRAGONS

The Chinese mathematician and astronomer Chang Heng designed this bronze seismoscope in about AD 130. Shock waves make the pendulum inside it swing, releasing a ball from a dragon's mouth. The direction of the earthquake source is shown by whichever toad catches a ball!

DANGEROUS WORK

An earthquake in Mexico, in 1985, toppled many tall buildings. This specially trained dog was used to sniff for survivors in the rubble. Aftershocks can make damaged structures even more unstable and too dangerous for rescuers. But sniffer dogs can tread lightly over the wreckage to locate trapped survivors.

21

TSUNAMI

TSUNAMIS ARE GIANT WAVES TRIGGERED BY volcanic eruptions and underwater earthquakes. They begin as broad, low ripples in the open sea, often passing unnoticed beneath ships. Although tsunamis start small, they are incredibly fast, travelling across deep water at more than 700 kmh (435 mph), the speed of a jet aircraft. When they reach shallow water, they slow down and begin rising to a terrifying size – sometimes up to 60 m (200 ft) high. Water is usually drawn away from the shore before a tsunami arrives, leaving fish stranded and wrecks exposed. People who come to look at these strange sights are often swept away when the wave suddenly rears up out of the sea.

NO ORDINARY WAVE

Tsunamis are not related to ordinary waves blown up by the wind. Wind waves are steep, narrow, and slow-moving. They are clearly visible as they cross the water. Tsunamis remain hidden until the last minute. They move by stealth, and are very hard to detect as they race over thousands of kilometres of sea. When they reach the shore, they are sometimes mistaken for tidal waves (caused by a tidal surge), although they have nothing to do with tides.

BIRTH OF A TSUNAMI

When seismic activity causes the seabed to rise or fall abruptly, the surrounding sea bulges and spreads out in a sequence of ripple-like waves. This can produce a series of tsunamis, one after the other. The ripples are usually very broad, and can reach more than 200 km (124 miles) in length, even though they may be less than 0.5 m (20 in) high in the open ocean.

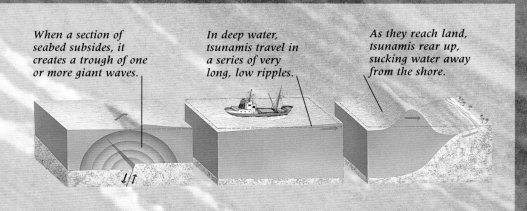

When a section of seabed subsides, it creates a trough of one or more giant waves.

In deep water, tsunamis travel in a series of very long, low ripples.

As they reach land, tsunamis rear up, sucking water away from the shore.

THE GOOD FRIDAY TSUNAMI

On Good Friday, 27 March 1964, a massive earthquake under the sea near Alaska, USA, sent a tsunami down the northwest Pacific coast. Alaskans were familiar with tsunamis, but the residents of Oregon and California were not. When the civil defence chief of Crescent City, California, received a tsunami warning, he had to seek advice to find out what a tsunami was! Later that day, Crescent City was struck by the wave, and 16 people died. Crescent City got off lightly. In 1883, a tsunami caused by the eruption of Karakatoa, Indonesia, killed 36,000 people.

HILO, HAWAII

This picture shows some of the devastation caused by a tsunami that struck Hilo, Hawaii, in 1946. The wave travelled 3,000 km (1,865 miles) from the coast of Alaska, taking five hours to reach Hilo Bay. The horseshoe shape of the bay funnelled the tsunami's force onto the town, killing 159 people. Today, the Pacific Tsunami Warning Centre, based on Hawaii, alerts coastal towns to unusually large sea waves.

JAPANESE WAVE

"Tsunami" is a Japanese word meaning harbour wave. This famous Japanese painting by Kanagawa shows a tsunami approaching Mt Fuji, on Japan's Honshu island. Japan is especially prone to tsunamis because it lies inside the Pacific "Ring of Fire" – a region surrounded by volcanoes and earthquake zones.

SPREADING SEAS

ABOUT 200 MILLION YEARS BEFORE HUMANS walked the Earth, today's continents were joined together in a single landmass that geologists call Pangaea. Over time, continental landmasses have slowly separated, drifted, and in some cases, collided. The original single ocean, called Panthalassa, has divided into the five oceans we see today. The continents continue to move, and the oceans change shape. Computer simulations suggest that in 250 million years time, the continents will once again come together in a single giant landmass. In the meantime, the Pacific Ocean is gradually shrinking and a new ocean is emerging in the Red Sea. New sea floor is being laid down at mid-ocean ridges, where volcanoes sometimes emerge, punching their way to the surface to form volcanic islands.

PILLOW LAVA
Along the mid-ocean ridges, lava squirts out through cracks. When it comes into contact with cold water, a glassy skin forms around the lava. This brittle surface splits and allows the still-molten lava inside to ooze out. Continued oozing and splitting produces rounded shapes resembling heaps of pillows – hence the lava's name. Pillow lava is made of basalt – the most common rock found on the Earth's surface.

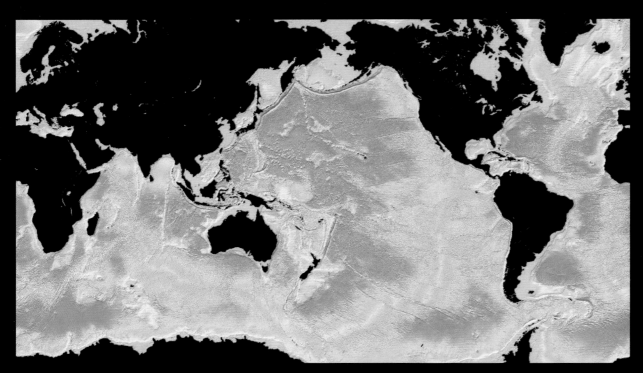

MID-OCEAN RIDGE SYSTEM
This computer-generated map, compiled from echosoundings and satellite data, depicts the contours of the sea floor. Shown here in yellow, the mid-ocean ridge system winds its way through the centre of the world's oceans. The ridge system is about 65,000 km (40,000 miles) long – more than three times the length of the Andes, Rockies, and Himalayas combined. Along its length, on either side, the Earth's tectonic plates move apart. Magma rises up within the ridge to fill the gaps, and so creates new sea floor.

RED SEA
This view of the northern end of the Red Sea shows the Gulf of Suez on the left and the Gulf of Aqaba on the right, with the Sinai desert in between. The Red Sea began to form about 20 million years ago when sea water flooded into the rift valley between Africa and Arabia. This rift is widening at the rate of about 2.5 cm (1 in) each year. In 100 million years time, the Red Sea may be the size of a mature ocean like the present-day Atlantic.

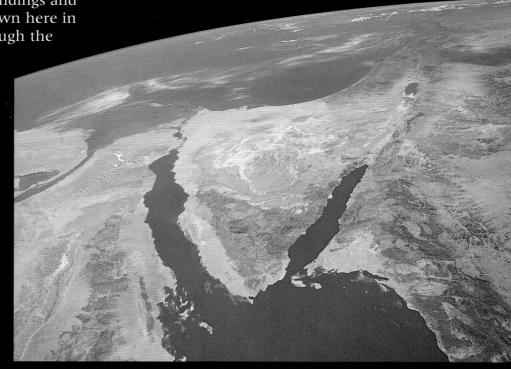

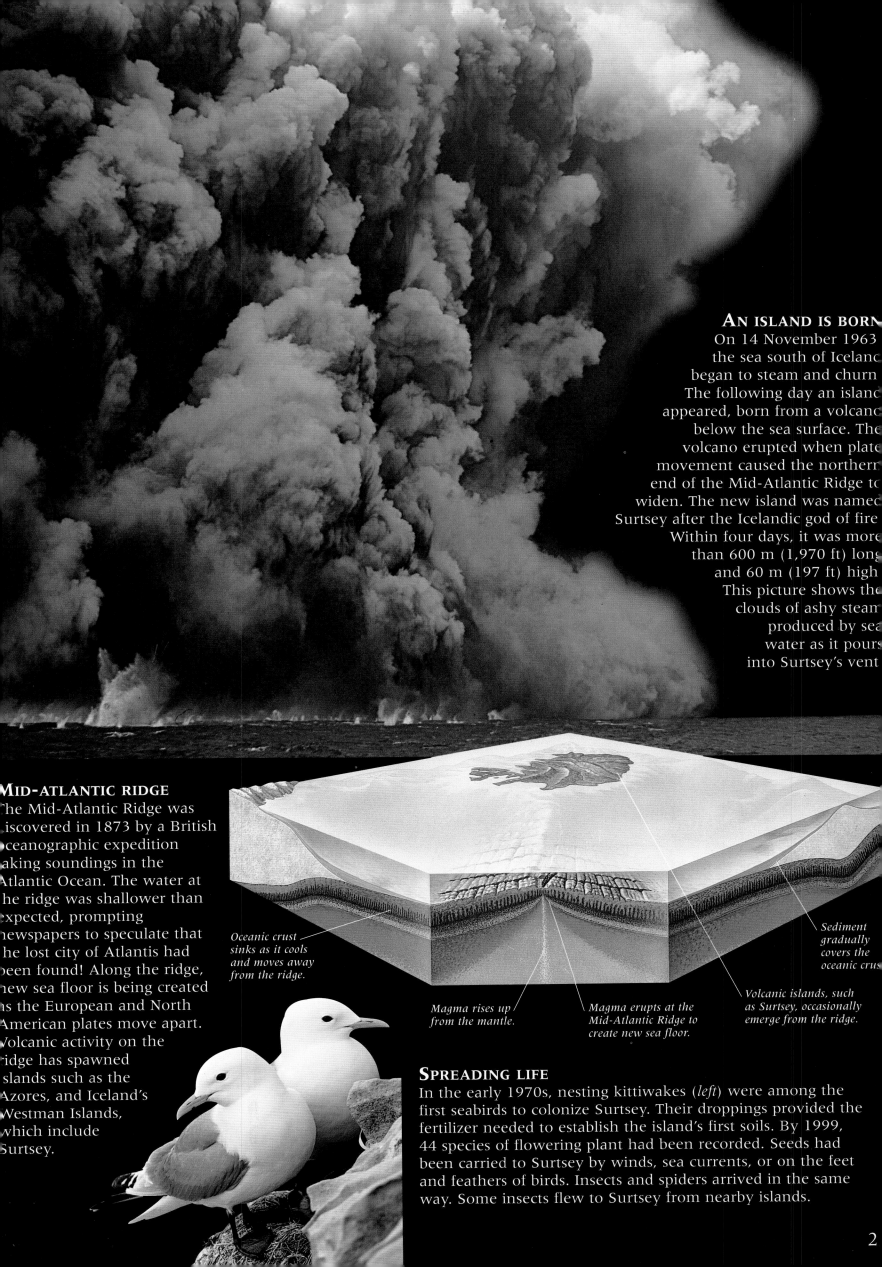

AN ISLAND IS BORN

On 14 November 1963 the sea south of Iceland began to steam and churn. The following day an island appeared, born from a volcano below the sea surface. The volcano erupted when plate movement caused the northern end of the Mid-Atlantic Ridge to widen. The new island was named Surtsey after the Icelandic god of fire. Within four days, it was more than 600 m (1,970 ft) long and 60 m (197 ft) high. This picture shows the clouds of ashy steam produced by sea water as it pours into Surtsey's vent.

MID-ATLANTIC RIDGE

The Mid-Atlantic Ridge was discovered in 1873 by a British oceanographic expedition taking soundings in the Atlantic Ocean. The water at the ridge was shallower than expected, prompting newspapers to speculate that the lost city of Atlantis had been found! Along the ridge, new sea floor is being created as the European and North American plates move apart. Volcanic activity on the ridge has spawned islands such as the Azores, and Iceland's Westman Islands, which include Surtsey.

Oceanic crust sinks as it cools and moves away from the ridge.

Magma rises up from the mantle.

Magma erupts at the Mid-Atlantic Ridge to create new sea floor.

Sediment gradually covers the oceanic crust

Volcanic islands, such as Surtsey, occasionally emerge from the ridge.

SPREADING LIFE

In the early 1970s, nesting kittiwakes (*left*) were among the first seabirds to colonize Surtsey. Their droppings provided the fertilizer needed to establish the island's first soils. By 1999, 44 species of flowering plant had been recorded. Seeds had been carried to Surtsey by winds, sea currents, or on the feet and feathers of birds. Insects and spiders arrived in the same way. Some insects flew to Surtsey from nearby islands.

2

SUBMARINE LANDSCAPES

THE OCEAN DEPTHS REMAIN MYSTERIOUS, even today. Sunlight penetrates to no more than a few hundred metres. Further down is an alien world of abyssal plains, mountains, and trenches inhabited by creatures rarely seen by humans. Until the 20th century, the only way to map the sea floor was by plumbing its depths with a weight and line. The invention of sonar – using sound waves to "see" – has revolutionized our knowledge of the sea floor. Scientists now know that the oceans hide many more volcanoes than are found on continents, and that the largest mountain ranges on Earth are found in the inky depths of the sea, not on land. However, the crushing pressure of deep water makes these places very difficult to visit.

LAUNCHING GLORIA

This torpedo-shaped sonar device, called GLORIA, is being launched from a research vessel. Towed behind the ship, it bounces sound waves off the sea floor. The returning signals are analysed to build up a 3-D map. This helps scientists to identify hazards on the sea bed, determine routes for laying cables, and locate areas for exploring minerals and oil.

MOUNTAINS AND TRENCHES

This map shows some of the rugged landscape of the sea floor. Long ridge systems of steep mountains, meander through the world's oceans. Some rise to more than 2 km (1.2 miles) above the sea floor. Elsewhere, ocean basins plunge into deep-sea trenches that are nearly 11,000 m (36,000 ft) below the surface – the deepest places on Earth.

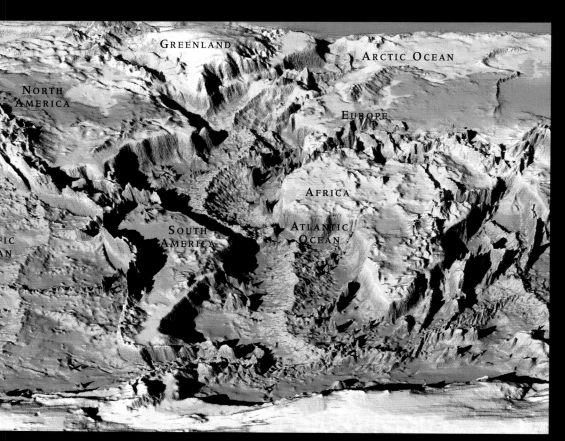

OCEAN FLOOR

Ocean basins are places where dense crust has settled down to form depressions filled with seawater. The ocean floor is the bottom of the basin. A continental slope marks the edge of the ocean basin and is the true geological boundary between continent and ocean. Giant cracks in the continental slope, or submarine canyons, deposit fans of sediment onto the basin. Underwater avalanches, called turbidity currents, occasionally rush down the canyon with such speed and power that they snap underwater telephone cables.

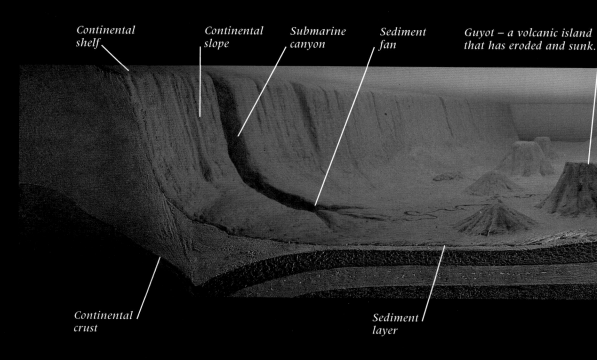

Continental shelf *Continental slope* *Submarine canyon* *Sediment fan* *Guyot – a volcanic island that has eroded and sunk.*

Continental crust *Sediment layer*

BLACK SMOKERS

On the deep sea floor, close to spreading ocean ridges, strange structures belch out clouds of volcanically heated water. They are hydrothermal vents, or "black smokers" (*left*). The sulphur-rich water coming from the smokers can be as hot as 400°C (752°F), but does not boil due to the immense pressure of the water. A mound of mineral deposits has built up around the vents, forming weird, chimney-like stacks.

RADIOLARIAN

DIATOMS

GIANT TUBE WORMS

In 1977, at a depth of 2,200 m (7,200 ft), scientists discovered an astonishing world of giant tube worms, growing in clusters around hydrothermal vents. The worms have no mouth or gut, but feed on the bacteria growing inside them. The bacteria break down chemicals from the vent water to make food for themselves and the worms. This startling discovery proved that not all life ultimately depends on the Sun's energy for food.

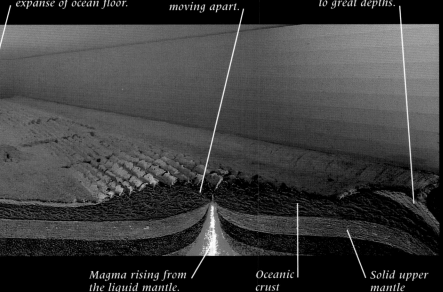

Abyssal plain – the flat expanse of ocean floor.

Spreading ridge, where two tectonic plates are moving apart.

Ocean trench plunging to great depths.

Magma rising from the liquid mantle.

Oceanic crust

Solid upper mantle

OOZE

These distorted discs are the silica skeletons of diatoms – single-celled algae that float in surface waters. Diatoms photosynthesize (trap light to make food), just as plants do on land. The spiny ball is a radiolarian – a single-celled animal that feeds on diatoms. When diatoms and radiolarians die, they sink to the sea bed to form a carpet of ooze that can be 500 m (1,640 ft) thick in places. The tiny organisms living in ooze feed a variety of bizarre creatures that have adapted to life in the darkness of the deep ocean.

27

WEATHERING AND EROSION

THE FOOTPRINTS LEFT BY ASTRONAUTS on the surface of the Moon in 1969 are still there today. The Moon, without an atmosphere, lacks weather. Footprints left in the Earth's dust are covered or swept away within days or even hours. This is because weather constantly shapes our planet's surface. Even solid rock does not last forever. When exposed, it becomes weathered. Assault by physical, chemical, and biological processes breaks it down, eventually turning even the hardest granite to soft clay. Erosion is the wearing down and removal of rock in the form of sediment. This can be rapid or gradual, depending on the type of rock.

AMMONITE GRAVEYARD
These are the fossilized remains of ammonites – sea creatures related to squid and cuttlefish. They died and were smothered in sediment some 65 million years ago. Their shells and the sediment surrounding them eventually turned to rock. Weathering and erosion have now uncovered these fossils in their ancient graves.

HOODOOS
In Goblin Valley, Utah, USA, strange pedestals of rock, called hoodoos (*right*), are shaped by wind, water, and temperature change. A sharp drop in temperature at night causes the rock surface to splinter. During the day, sand-blasting winds carve out eerie shapes. Where the rock is resistant, a bulging head or belly forms. Where the rock succumbs more easily to erosion, a waist or neck develops.

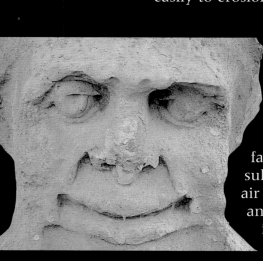

ACID RAIN
This limestone sculpture has been disfigured by acid rain. The natural, weak acidity of rainwater has been strengthened by pollution. Traffic fumes and factory smoke contain oxides of sulphur and nitrogen. These react with air and rainwater to make sulphuric and nitric acids. When the acids fall in rain, they dissolve limestone, and damage trees and lake life.

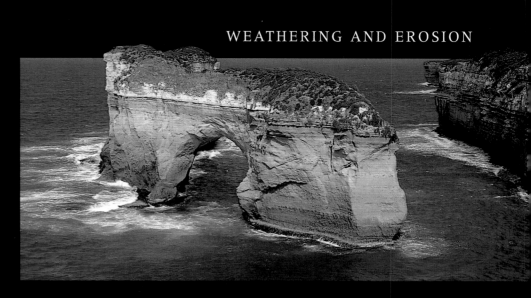

SEA EROSION

This naturally carved sandstone arch in Western Victoria, Australia, demonstrates the immense power of wind, waves, and currents to cut through solid rock. Waves wear away coastal rocks by pounding them with water, hurling stones at them, and forcing air into cracks so hard that the rocks burst apart. When the arch eventually collapses, it may leave behind spectacular tall pillars of rock called stacks.

NIAGARA FALLS

Waterfalls occur where there is an abrupt change in land level during a river's journey from source to sea. Flowing water will erode any soft rocks at the waterfall's edge or in the plunge pool at its base. Where harder rocks remain, creating rocky outcrops, steep rapids may appear. The Niagara Falls, on the USA's border with Canada, flow over hard limestone, which overlays a softer sandstone. The Falls are eroding the rock at the rate of 1 m (3 ft 3 in) a year. So far, the Falls have cut back the rock by 11 km (7 miles).

PLANT ATTACK

Plants speed up the weathering process by penetrating cracks in rocks. As this tree grows, its roots thicken and reach deeper into the rocky ground. Slowly, the roots widen the cracks and the rocks split further. Animals add to the process by burrowing through the cracks, and mosses dissolve the rocks' surfaces with plant acids.

GRAND CANYON

The majestic Grand Canyon in Arizona, USA, was carved by the Colorado River over a period of 20 million years. The river has eroded its way down to rock that is two billion years old. Wind, frost, rain, and tumbling streams have all shaped the canyon's sides. The rocks in various layers respond in different ways to the forces of erosion. Hard sandstones produce cliffs, soft shales form slopes. This creates the canyon's rich mix of shape and texture.

CAVES AND CAVERNS

FOR MANY PEOPLE, THE DARKNESS OF DRIPPING CAVES hides the threat of the unknown. But an underground place can also be a safe refuge, and for thousands of years, humans made their homes in caves. The action of lava, ice, and waves can form a cave, but the most spectacular results occur where limestone is eroded by rainwater. This can produce vast caverns full of strange rock formations. When water absorbs carbon dioxide from the air or soil, it becomes slightly acidic and dissolves limestone, which is porous and erodes more easily than harder rocks such as granite. The process is very gradual. It can take 100,000 years for flowing water to carve a cave only 3 m (10 ft) deep. But the bigger the cave becomes, the more rapidly it is eroded, until eventually the water leaves a system of tunnels and caverns.

VANISHING STREAMS
Where streams disappear through gaps in the ground, they may erode the rock to form great shafts called swallow-holes. At Gaping Gill Cave in Yorkshire, England, a stream falls 110 m (361 ft) through a swallow-hole in the roof of a vast limestone cavern. This unbroken waterfall, and the cavern below it, are the largest of their kind in Britain. Gaping Gill is part of a system of caves that extends for more than 60 km (37 miles).

CHINESE KARST
The Guilin Hills in southwest China are fine examples of a limestone scenery called karst. Heavy rain, high humidity, and rich plant growth combine to produce plenty of acidic surface water. The acid's erosion of the limestone, in a process called carbonation, has sculpted a dramatic landscape. These porous, stony hills lack streams, because all water permeates the rock to create honeycombs of caves and caverns.

CAVE FORMATIONS
Dripping water has created these beautiful, multicoloured cave formations in Nevada, USA. Water percolating through the limestone has dissolved calcium carbonate and different coloured minerals, such as iron, to form long, icicle-shaped deposits called stalactites, which hang from the ceiling. Where water drips from the stalactite, some carbonate falls to the floor and builds up a candle-like pinnacle called a stalagmite. It can take several thousand years for a stalagmite to grow just 2.5 cm (1 in).

CAVE BATS
These endangered ghost bats roost near the entrances of caves in Australia. They emerge at night to hunt insects and small animals. Like most other cave-dwelling animals, these bats use senses other than sight to locate their food. By emitting high-pitched squeaks, and listening like radar to the returning echoes, the bats can build up a "sound picture" of their surroundings.

COLLAPSE!
People sometimes build on karst landscapes with disastrous results. Limestone caverns may form just a few metres below the surface, and heavy rain can cause a cavern's ceiling to collapse. This happened in Winterpark, Florida, USA, in 1981, when a house and six parked cars plunged into a previously unknown cavern. The hole reached 200 m (656 ft) across and 50 m (164 ft) deep.

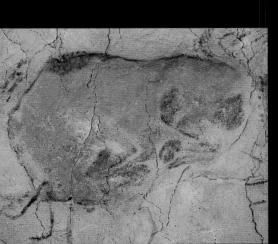

CAVE HOME
This painting of a crouching bison, with its head between its front hooves, is at least 15,000 years old. Discovered in 1869 by a hunter entering Altamira Cave, northern Spain, it is one of dozens of vivid animal images on the walls and ceilings of the cave. The paintings depict the hunting life of the cave dwellers.

31

ICY EXTREMES

THE PLACES MOST HOSTILE TO HUMAN LIFE ARE FOUND at the ends of the Earth. Polar ice caps cover the Arctic at the North Pole, and Antarctica at the South Pole, keeping them icy all year round. Yet the two regions differ in an important respect. The Arctic is a frozen ocean bordered by continents, but Antarctica is a continent surrounded by the Southern Ocean. Both places are further from the Sun than the rest of the world. Because the Earth rotates at an angle, the Arctic is plunged from total darkness during the winter to constant daylight during the summer, as the North Pole moves nearer to or away from the Sun. But despite the low temperatures, polar regions are teeming with wildlife that has adapted to the intense cold. Seals and whales thrive in the freezing waters, protected by thick blubber. Bears are a common sight on Arctic ice, as birds are in Antarctica.

CARIBOU TRAIL

These North American caribou, or reindeer, migrate northwards in the summer to graze on the grasses, shrubs, and mosses uncovered by the melting ice of the Arctic tundra. Unlike other deer, caribou migrate in large herds, and both males and females have antlers.

ARCTIC OCEAN

All year round, more than half of the Arctic Ocean is covered in sea ice to a depth of at least 3 m (10 ft). In summer, some of the ice melts and breaks up to create ice floes like those shown here. For centuries, explorers believed that the Arctic ice lay over a vast continent. In 1958, a nuclear submarine sailed right under the ice cap and proved that this was untrue.

ARCTIC POLAR BEAR

The largest predators in the Arctic roam across the ice floes hunting seals, their favourite food. Polar bears are well adapted to Arctic life. Layers of blubber keep them warm, creamy white fur provides camouflage when hunting, and hollow hairs provide buoyancy in the water. Polar bears have non-slip soles to grip the ice, and partially webbed feet. They can swim for many hours in the freezing sea.

ICEBERG, DEAD AHEAD!

Icebergs are giant chunks of floating ice that break away, or calve, from ice sheets or glaciers. Most of their mass lies hidden below sea level. This berg, newly broken away from the Antarctic ice shelf, is flat-topped. Storm waves have not yet eroded it into sharp pinnacles. Antarctic icebergs can be enormous. The biggest ever recorded had a sea area larger than Belgium.

ANTARCTIC PENGUINS

These young Emperor penguins, with their mothers, are several months old. In autumn, adults gather on Antarctica to pair and mate. The female lays a single egg that she passes to the male. Throughout the Antarctic winter, when temperatures can plummet to −50°C (−58°F), the male incubates the egg on his feet, which nestle under a warm flap of skin. The female returns when the egg hatches, and takes over parenting duties.

STUDYING ANTARCTICA

This scientist is slicing an ice core drilled from the Antarctic ice cap. The core is a time capsule containing trapped air from thousands of years ago. Analysis will reveal what the Earth's atmosphere was once like. It tells scientists how naturally occurring greenhouse gases may have caused global warming in the past. The information may help us to predict what might happen in the future.

GLACIERS

At the North and South Poles, and in high mountain regions, immense glaciers are shaping the landscape. Glaciers are titanic rivers of snow and ice. They move slowly and are easily deflected, but their sheer weight and size give them enormous strength. As glaciers creep forwards, they dislodge and carry away gravel and boulders that scratch and grind the rocks beneath. Wide valleys are carved, great bowls are gouged in the mountainside, and entire hills are sliced away in a glacier's relentless advance. During the last Ice Age, northern glaciers and ice-sheets extended across much of Europe and North America. However, over the past 10,000 years, many glaciers have shrunk or become shorter because they are melting faster than they are replenished with snow.

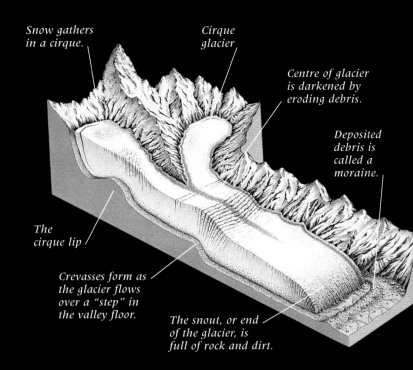

Snow gathers in a cirque.

Cirque glacier

Centre of glacier is darkened by eroding debris.

Deposited debris is called a moraine.

The cirque lip

Crevasses form as the glacier flows over a "step" in the valley floor.

The snout, or end of the glacier, is full of rock and dirt.

THE MAKING OF A GLACIER

An Alpine valley glacier (*above*) forms when snow gathers in high-altitude basins, called cirques. Further snowfall feeds the glacier, until its ice becomes thick and compacted. Slowly, it begins to move under the pressure of its own weight, and grinds against the valley sides, collecting rocks as it goes. When it reaches lower ground the glacier melts and deposits rocky debris.

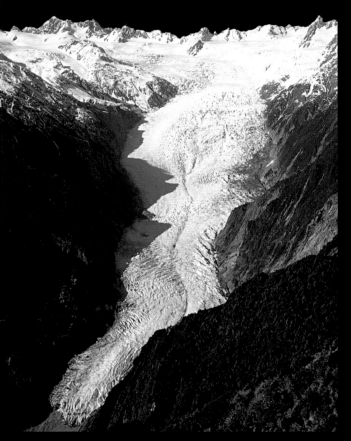

FRANZ JOSEF GLACIER

This glacier in New Zealand's Southern Alps is probably the world's fastest. It often reaches speeds of 7 m (23 ft) a day during summer. Giant cracks, or crevasses, are clearly visible where the brittle surface has fractured. This happens where the glacier rises over a bump or is deflected around a bend. Crevasses are treacherous. Often many metres deep, they can swallow an unwary walker.

NORWEGIAN FJORD

This Norwegian fjord was carved by glaciers about two million years ago, during the last Ice Age. Fjords are long, deep-sea inlets gouged out by glaciers. Most formed in existing V-shaped river valleys, which were made U-shaped by the glacier's erosion. Some are as deep as 1,000 m (3,280 ft). A fjord's mouth is sometimes shallower, where the glacier began to float in the sea and its erosive power was reduced. When the ice melted, the sea level rose, and flooded the fjords.

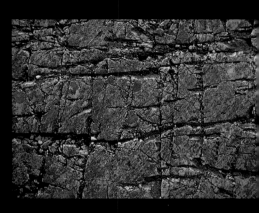

GLACIER MARKS
Wherever they go, glaciers leave their tell-tale marks. We know that many landscapes in today's temperate regions were carved by glaciers, because exposed rocks have been polished flat by moving ice. In areas such as Scotland's Highlands, deep grooves (*right*), called striations, have been scoured into the valley sides by the passing rocks embedded in a long-vanished glacier.

SLIP, SLIDING AWAY
At Gilkey Glacier, Alaska, USA, three glaciers meet. Rock scraped away from the valley sides darkens the glaciers' edges, and reveals movement. A glacier flows fastest in its central section. The outer edges move more slowly, held back by friction with the valley sides. Glaciers speed up in summer because their undersides melt, making them slide along more easily.

THE HUBBARD GLACIER
In 1986, the enormous Hubbard Glacier in Alaska suddenly speeded up. It normally travels at 5 cm (2 in) a day, but for one month it sped along at 45 m (148 ft) a day, and blocked off the Russell Fjord in Yakutat Bay. Seals, sea lions, and porpoises became trapped in a seawater lake behind the ice. The lake gradually became brackish as melt water entered from the glacier. The animals finally escaped when the glacier retreated.

35

AVALANCHE!

WITH A THUNDEROUS ROAR, YOUR FEET are swept from under you, and you gasp for air as snow fills your mouth. You are caught in an avalanche – a massive collapse of snow that sweeps down a mountainside. The slide is often caused by a thaw melting a buried layer of snow, making the snow on top liable to slip. Vibrations, caused by a loud noise or ground tremor, then trigger the collapse. Avalanches are not the only sliding danger. A landslide is a slippage of unstable rock or soil triggered by heavy rainfall, or by a violent earthquake or volcano. Between them, avalanches and landslides claim thousands of lives a year.

HELICOPTER
RESCUE

AVALANCHE DESTRUCTION

This is the scene of devastation after avalanches struck the towns of Galtur and Valzur in Austria, in February 1999. Snowslides, triggered by snowstorms and high winds, swept away cars and sliced through buildings, killing 38 people. The damage was severe because local authorities had not installed avalanche defences around Galtur. No fatal snowslides had occurred in the area since 1689. Helicopters ferried people away from the disaster area, but fewer than a third of those buried in the snowslides survived.

AVALANCHE BARRIERS

Various measures can be taken to prevent or lessen the impact of an avalanche. In mountainous regions, such as the European Alps, planting trees or building avalanche barriers (*right*) can halt or deflect dangerous snowslides. Experts even use explosives to trigger controlled avalanches before dangerous ones can occur.

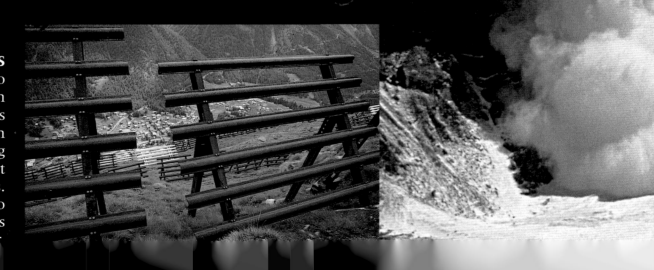

AVALANCHE IN PROGRESS

In an avalanche, the main mass of snow can travel at speeds of up to 95 kmh (60 mph). During its onrush, the avalanche uproots trees, flips vehicles, and topples buildings. People are crushed or buried. The snow then sets like concrete, and buried people suffocate or freeze to death. The worst avalanche in recent history occurred in the Andes in 1970. An earthquake triggered an avalanche and landslide on Peru's Huascarán mountain, and claimed 20,000 lives.

MUDSLIDE

A mudslide is a very wet landslide. Soil, mixed with water from heavy rain or melting snow, becomes a liquid, and flows much faster and further than an ordinary landslide. In December 1999, torrential rains unleashed tides of mud, trees, and boulders that swept through coastal towns near Caracas, Venezuela (*above*). Over five days, more than 15,000 people were smothered or battered to death by mudslides. Some 100,000 people were made homeless.

UNCERTAIN FUTURE

Global warming seems to make weather more extreme, with unexpected storms and thaws triggering dangerous avalanches and landslides. The impact of these slips is being felt more because people are becoming more mobile. Mountain roads are prone to landslides (*above*), and more people are visiting snow-covered mountains for leisure, where the danger of avalanches is highest.

AMONG THE MOST DESOLATE PLACES ON EARTH are the deserts. About 15 per cent of our planet's land surface is covered in true desert, and this ratio is gradually increasing. Some deserts are hot and dry all year round, others are dry with intensely cold winters. The cold lands of the Arctic and Antarctic are also deserts. What they have in common is a lack of water. A desert is an area that receives less than 25 cm (10 in) of rain in an average year, though years may go by when no rain falls at all. The air over a desert may be very dry or cold, or both, so any surface water quickly evaporates or freezes. Even hot deserts can be bitterly cold at night. Clear skies trap little heat and by morning there may be dew on the ground – a vital source of moisture for plants and animals that live in the desert.

PRICKLY GIANT

The saguaro cactus of the southwestern USA, is marvellously adapted to desert life. This plant takes 200 years to grow to a height of 15 m (49 ft). Its roots reach out 18 m (59 ft) in search of water, which it can store in its thick, cork-covered stem. Instead of leaves, cactuses have sharp spines. These reduce water loss through evaporation, and deter grazing animals.

RAIN-FREE ZONE

A typical year in Chile's Atacama Desert means no rainfall at all. In 1971, parts of the Atacama received rain for the first time in 400 years. Cold ocean currents off South America cool the wind as it blows onto land. Any moisture turns to fog at the coast, so very little reaches the desert. This makes the Atacama one of the driest places on Earth.

DUNE SEA

When people think of deserts, they imagine dunes – hills of loose sand blown by the wind. In fact, only about 20 per cent of the world's deserts are sandy. Most are wildernesses of rock and stone. Where a desert is mainly sand – such as here, in the Namib Desert of southwest Africa – the wind creates large drifts and dunes, some of which can be 500 m (1,640 ft) tall. Sand is blown up the shallow side of a dune and tumbles down the steep side. Grain by grain, the dune drifts, like a slow-moving wave on a great dune sea.

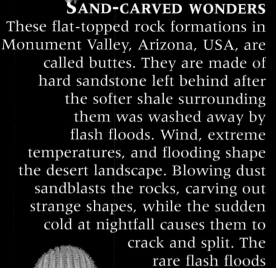

SAND-CARVED WONDERS

These flat-topped rock formations in Monument Valley, Arizona, USA, are called buttes. They are made of hard sandstone left behind after the softer shale surrounding them was washed away by flash floods. Wind, extreme temperatures, and flooding shape the desert landscape. Blowing dust sandblasts the rocks, carving out strange shapes, while the sudden cold at nightfall causes them to crack and split. The rare flash floods cut deep gorges and channels.

BADLANDS

Badlands are barren, dry, and hilly. Their terrain is inhospitable, and difficult to walk upon. French explorers dubbed them "bad lands to cross," hence the name. These regions have a desert-like appearance, but receive more rain than most true deserts. Often, badlands are made by people. Poor farming practices can remove the vegetation that binds soil together. Flash floods then wash the loosened soil away, turning fertile land into a dry wasteland. This process is known as desertification. These badlands in Alberta, Canada, formed naturally when flash floods carved drainage channels in the soft clay and rocks.

TRAPPING MOISTURE

Although deserts are expanding in some places, they are disappearing in others. Here, in Israel's Dead Sea region, farmers are irrigating watermelon plants with piped water. The plants are protected by plastic sheeting, which reduces water evaporation. By drip-feeding water to individual plants, farmers can cultivate barren land and make it bloom.

DROUGHT

HOT, DRY WEATHER IS A BLESSING TO SOME, and a deadly curse to others. Continued lack of rain causes drought – a temporary water shortage – and without water, life eventually dries up. Water shortages in wealthy nations may only cause hose pipe bans, but in developing countries, the effects of drought kill thousands of people each year. If drought conditions persist, plants wilt, crops fail, and domestic animals die. Without clean water, or plants and animals for food, people die too. Poor farming practices – such as removing trees and growing crops that do not bind the soil – mean that the land does not retain moisture. This, along with climate change and overpopulation, continues to make droughts a devastating global problem.

DUST BOWL

Blinding dust storms occur where light, parched soil is whipped up by the wind, such as here in the Australian outback (*left*). In the American midwest of the 1930s, years of cattle grazing and wheat growing had made the soil fine and crumbly. After a long drought, the ploughed fields turned to dust and were blown away in huge brown clouds. By 1937, about half a million people had abandoned the region.

SPREADING DESERT

Water is scarce in deserts, such as the Namib in southwest Africa, because circulating air masses create a very dry climate. At the fringes of this desert, slight changes in air circulation can bring moist air and rain one year, but none the next. Overgrazing and climate change make the area even drier, turning it into a barren expanse of cracked mud and dead trees.

FAMINE

Between the 1960s and early 1980s, the area south of the Sahara Desert in Africa received almost no rain. Crops failed, and by 1985, hundreds of thousands of Ethiopians were dying from starvation and a lack of clean water. The situation was made worse by a civil war that ravaged the country's economy. Live Aid, a global charity concert, raised money to send food, clothing, shelter, and medical supplies to Ethiopia's starving people.

EL NIÑO

El Niño is the name of a seasonal warm-water current (shown in red) that occurs off the coast of Peru. The El Niño current occurs every five to seven years when the winds temporarily change direction over the Pacific Ocean. In some years, a strong change drives warm water east towards South America, making the air more humid and causing violent storms. At the same time, countries in the western Pacific, deprived of warm ocean currents, have very dry weather. The El Niño of 1997–98, shown in this computer image, was one of the strongest on record. It brought droughts to Australia, India, and Southeast Asia.

LOST CIVILIZATION

Chaco Canyon in New Mexico, USA, is almost a desert. Yet a thousand years ago, this area supported a thriving Native American civilization – the Anasazi. For hundreds of years the inhabitants cut down trees for building and firewood. Then, when a drought occurred, the remaining vegetation was unable to retain water in the soil, and crops and other plants died. The Anasazi left, and today the ruins of their civilization lie in the dust.

Curled up in its moist burrow, this air-breathing African lungfish can survive out of water for several months.

LUNGFISH

Each summer, rivers in parts of Africa dry up and become roads of baked mud. When the autumn rains fall, the rivers spring back to life. Lungfish live through the drought by curling up in mucus-lined burrows dug into the riverbed. They can survive for a whole summer with no extra food or water, and very little air.

41

FOREST FIRES

ALONG, HOT SUMMER, dry grass, and a lightning strike are all it takes to start a forest fire. Very high temperatures can even cause the natural oils in dry plants to burst spontaneously into flame. About half of all forest fires start naturally like this. The rest are started by people – deliberately or accidentally. Once a fire starts, it has a life of its own. Flames leap from tree to tree, burning embers are tossed into the air and start new fires, and rising heat sucks in air at ground level, fanning the flames. Temperatures in the inferno can reach well above 500°C (932°F). In minutes, wildlife may be wiped out and the landscape transformed.

FOREST FIRE-FIGHTER

Firefighters on the ground hose a bushfire with water, or spray foams that starve the flames of oxygen and fuel. Other tactics include removing vegetation ahead of the fire, either by controlled burning or by cutting and digging a firebreak. Despite advances in technology, containing a forest fire remains expensive and dangerous, and often involves hundreds of firefighters.

Firefighters wear brightly coloured, fire-resistant clothing.

FIRE-FIGHTING PLANE

Firefighters try to control a fire by lowering its temperature and cutting off its supply of oxygen. In hard-to-reach places, such as here in British Columbia, Canada, planes are used to drench the blaze with water and special chemicals. This reduces the fire's heat. Planes also douse the vegetation in the fire's path, making it less likely to catch fire.

BUSHFIRE IN CALIFORNIA

In late 1993, raging wildfires swept through southern California, USA, forcing 25,000 people to evacuate their homes. After six years of drought, dry timber caught fire easily. The fires spread rapidly, fanned by 80 kmh (50 mph) winds. About 15,000 firefighters finally halted the flames on the outskirts of Los Angeles.

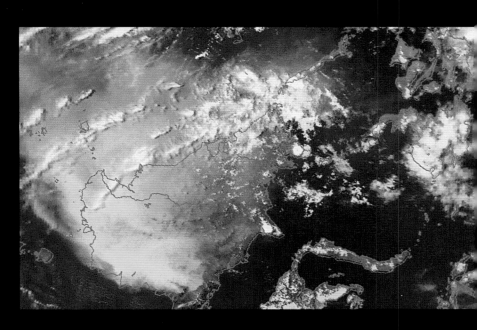

INDONESIA BURNING

In 1997, farmers in Indonesia carried out a clearance burning
that escaped their control. The yellow colour on this satellite
image shows a pall of smoke covering the country. When
it reached the cities, the smoke turned into thick smog, which
caused chaos. People had difficulty breathing, and poor visibility
caused a jetliner to crash in Sumatra, killing all on board.

SLASH AND BURN

In tropical South America and Southeast Asia,
farmers cut or burn down tracts of rainforest to clear
space for crops or cattle-rearing. Burning is a quick
way to clear the ground. However, the new land is
usually fertile only for a few years. Without its thick
tree cover and binding roots, the soil is leached of
its nutrients or washed away by heavy rain.

REGROWTH

Natural fires are not all bad news.
Fires kill pests, clear space, and
return nutrients to the soil. In North
America, lodgepole pines (*above*) only
release their seeds after a fire. Their
saplings exploit the nutrient-rich ash
and absence of competing trees.

CLIMATE CHANGE

THE 1990s WERE THE NORTHERN HEMISPHERE'S warmest decade on record. Most scientists now believe that the Earth's climate is rapidly warming and that humans are to blame. Some of the Sun's heat bounces off the Earth, and travels out through the atmosphere in the form of infrared radiation. Certain gases, such as carbon dioxide, absorb infrared radiation and trap heat in the atmosphere. This occurs naturally and is called the greenhouse effect. But burning fossil fuels to provide power for homes, industry, and cars produces extra carbon dioxide. This accelerates the greenhouse effect and overheats the planet. Other polluting gases are responsible for thinning the atmosphere's ozone layer, which shields us from harmful ultraviolet radiation.

HOLE IN THE OZONE

The ozone layer protects the Earth's living organisms from the Sun's harmful ultraviolet radiation. The deep blue area on this computer-generated view of the Earth in 2000 (*right*), indicates a gigantic hole in the ozone layer above Antarctica. Gases called CFCs (chlorofluorocarbons), which are used in refrigerators and aerosol sprays, have risen into the atmosphere and destroyed ozone. Many countries have now banned the use of CFCs, and the hole may now be getting smaller.

APOLLO BUTTERFLIES FROM THE EUROPEAN ALPINE MEADOWS FACE EXTINCTION

ADAPT OR DIE

When climate changes abruptly, animals and plants that cannot withstand or adapt to the new conditions must leave or face extinction. The Apollo butterfly has adapted to the cool climates of mountains. If global warming makes its habitat too warm, it will have nowhere left to go.

HOT AND CHOKED

On a sunny day, many big cities are covered in a choking brown smog (*left*). Smog is produced when gases from vehicle exhausts react with sunlight. The result is a thick haze that contains carbon monoxide and other harmful gases. Governments meet regularly to decide what can be done to reduce greenhouse gas emissions, but it seems to be too little too late to prevent global warming.

ICE RIFT

Since the mid-1990s, giant cracks have been appearing in parts of Antarctica's Larsen Ice Shelf, (*right*) and massive ice chunks have been floating away. This may be because more polar ice is melting. In sub-Antarctica, some penguin populations are declining as sea ice reduces because they have to swim further to find fish to eat.

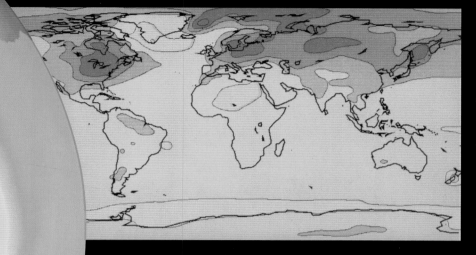

GLOBAL WARMING

If carbon dioxide and other greenhouse gases continue to pour into the atmosphere unchecked, the world may warm rapidly. This computer forecast (*above*) shows how much temperatures may increase by 2010 compared with temperatures in 1950. The red areas indicate a predicted increase of 4–5°C (7.2–9°F). Moderate rises are shown in orange. The pale areas indicate no change. Weather will probably become more unpredictable and extreme – with heavier rain in some places, and droughts in others.

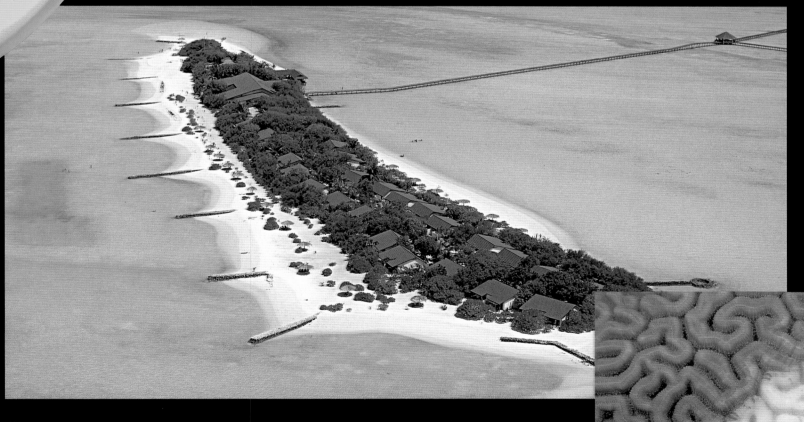

Unbleached coral containing algae

WATER TOO WARM

In 1998, whole coral reefs in the Indian Ocean turned white and died when water temperatures rose just 1–2°C (1.8–3.6°F) above normal. Reef-building corals are animals containing tiny algae that make food for the corals. If the waters become too warm, the corals eject the algae and die. A strong El Niño, perhaps enhanced by global warming, caused the temperature rise.

Bleached coral without algae

CLOSE-UP OF DAMAGED CORAL, INDIAN OCEAN

EXTREME WEATHER

THE SWIRLING, CHAOTIC MOVEMENT OF THE EARTH'S oceans and atmosphere is powered by the Sun. Tropical regions receive more sunlight than the poles and this heat imbalance causes air masses to shift. Warm air from tropical regions moves towards the North and South Poles and cool air returns. The oceans act as a massive heat store, and the interaction of ocean currents and air masses is complex and constantly changing. Heat energy from the oceans, transferred to the atmosphere, can unleash savage weather, producing hurricanes that demolish seaside communities, tornadoes that hurl cars into the air, and lightning strikes that split trees and melt sand. Depending where you live, extreme weather may be a regular feature, visiting every year, or it may be a rare event. But as global warming stirs the weather machine, extreme weather is probably becoming more common – wherever you live.

THE WEATHER MACHINE

The Sun's heat evaporates water from sea and land, and makes moist air rise. As warm air ascends into cooler levels of the atmosphere, its moisture condenses to form clouds. These drift in the wind until they evaporate or dump their water as rain, hail, or snow. The rotation of the Earth swirls winds around low pressure, rising air systems. Such winds swirl anti-clockwise in the northern hemisphere as seen (*top right*) in this satellite image.

HURRICANE HARASSMENT

In September 1998, Hurricane George hit the coast of Florida, USA, with winds of 145 kmh (90 mph). An estimated 600 people were killed. Hurricanes are powerful, rotating storms that form above warm, tropical seas. Their high wind speeds uproot trees, topple buildings, and fling boats ashore. The accompanying surge of seawater floods coastal regions, and torrential rain inundates inland areas. Hurricanes occur over the Atlantic Ocean. The same weather phenomena are called typhoons in the Pacific, and cyclones in the Indian Ocean. They regularly cause devastation and flooding in the Caribbean, the southeastern United States, and in the Asian countries bordering the Bay of Bengal.

Lightning strike

Few weather phenomena are as dramatic as lightning. A lightning flash is a giant electric spark generated by a storm. As ice and water rise and fall inside a cloud, they rub together and generate static electricity. Different parts of the cloud become highly charged. They eventually discharge to create lightning that flashes among the clouds or shoots down to Earth. Forked lightning (*left*) momentarily heats soil to about 1,800°C (3,300°F) when it touches the ground. People struck by lightning may die from burns or heart failure, but some survive. Park ranger Roy Sullivan of Virginia, USA, was reputedly struck on seven separate occasions!

Tornado terror

Tornadoes are narrow spiralling updrafts of air generated below giant thunderstorm clouds. The widest tornadoes contain winds that travel at more than 400 kmh (250 mph). Their power can be awesome, sweeping up people and buildings, derailing trains, and plucking herds of cattle from fields. The central states of the USA are lashed by dozens of tornadoes each year. In 1925, a cluster of tornadoes rampaged across Missouri, Illinois, and Indiana killing 689 people. An unseasonal tornado cluster swept through Georgia, USA, in February 2000, injuring about 100 people and killing 18.

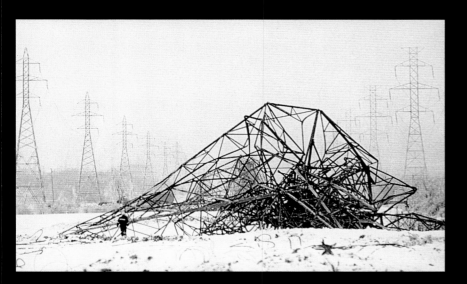

Iceball

Hailstones form in the high-altitude updrafts of thunderclouds, where water droplets cool and freeze together, and then fall from the sky. Large hailstones can sometimes hit the ground at 140 kmh (90 mph), but rarely kill people. Instead they damage buildings, vehicles, and crops. About 2 per cent of the USA's agricultural harvest is lost to hail each year. The largest hailstone on record fell in Kansas, USA, in September 1970. It weighed 766 g (27 oz) – more than twice the weight of this one.

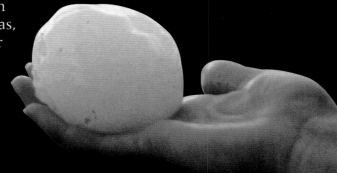

Big freeze

An unusual clash of air masses triggered the Canadian ice storm of January 1998. A layer of warm air in the atmosphere trapped cold air below, creating a temperature inversion. When rain fell it froze and coated the landscape in thick ice. The weight of ice brought trees and electrical pylons crashing down. In Quebec Province alone, more than three million people lost their electricity supply, 17,000 were forced from their homes, and cold or injury killed 30.

FLOODS

THE GREAT FLOOD DESCRIBED IN THE BIBLE may have been the earliest and greatest flood to beset humanity. However, flood myths are common to more than 250 cultures. Floods bring both destruction and renewal. Apart from disease, floods remain the worst of nature's disasters and are occurring more frequently as our climate changes. They bring the highest death toll and the greatest damage to property. The mud left by floodwater fills houses and sets like concrete. But floods have their advantages too. The mud that covers fields gives nutrients to the soil, and great civilizations have been founded on the fertile floodplains of the world's major rivers.

High tides threaten low-lying cities in northern Europe.

Monsoons cause flooding around the Bay of Bengal.

NORTH AMERICA

EUROPE

ATLANTIC OCEAN

ASIA

River flooding affects areas of southeasten USA.

AFRICA

PACIFIC OCEAN

INDIAN OCEAN

SOUTH AMERICA

Every year the Amazon River bursts its banks during the wet season.

AU

El Niño causes storm floods on the Pacific coast of South America.

Wet-season floods can affect parts of central Africa.

Tropical storms can cause flooding in northern Australia.

ANNUAL RAINFALL

■ More than 2,000 mm (78 in)   ■ 500–2,000 mm (20–78 in)   □ Less than 500 mm

KENYA UNDERWATER

The intense El Niño of 1997–98 brought storms, torrential rain, and flooding to many places, including Florida, California, Brazil, and Kenya. In parts of Kenya's savannah (*right*), the rainfall was more than five times the normal October–December average,causing floods that took weeks to subside. Afterwards, deaths from water-borne diseases, such as dysentery, rose steeply.

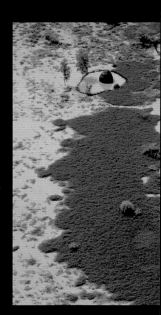

MISSISSIPPI FLOODING

The Mississippi, in the American midwest, is one of the world's largest rivers. Torrential rain fell in the region in 1993, causing massive runoff in parts where ground water was still high from previous years' rain. Flood defences had not been tested by such a surge of water and failed. The Mississippi and Missouri Rivers inundated more than 80,000 sq km (31,000 sq miles) of land, killing 48 people, and causing damage worth US$15 billion.

FLOOD RISK

Some regions of the world suffer more floods than others. Tropical areas get pounded by Monsoon rains and tropical storms. Inland valleys and floodplains are at risk if there is a build-up of rainwater or melting snow. Low-lying coastal areas can be affected by storm surges, unusually high tides and tsunamis. Estuaries suffer the worst of both worlds – they can be inundated by water from land or sea.

ANIMAL SHELTER

In Cambodia, cattle shelter on a tiny patch of ground to escape the floodwaters of the swollen Mekong River (*left*). Cambodia, with its wet climate and wide Mekong floodplain, floods dangerously every one to three years. Uncontrolled flooding disrupts whole communities by destroying homes and businesses, triggering food shortages, and increasing the risk of disease.

FLOOD MISERY

Here, Bangladeshi families struggle to rescue belongings from their flooded homes. Bangladesh straddles the delta of two of the mightiest rivers in Asia – the Ganges and the Brahmaputra. When the heavy monsoon rains fell in 1998, the swollen rivers inundated the country and made 30 million people homeless.

RIVER BARRIER

The Thames Barrier's steel-clad piers stand like helmeted soldiers across the River Thames in London. Completed in 1982, the barrier's raised gates protect the city from floods. A high tide, coinciding with strong winds, can produce tidal surges that travel upriver, threatening the capital. The barrier holds back such surges. Sea level rises may require the barrier to be strengthened by 2030.

DROWNING WORLD

IF THE EARTH CONTINUES TO WARM, more
polar ice will melt and sea levels will
rise. This could be a catastrophe for
people living in low-lying coastal areas.
But rising sea levels are nothing new.
Land and sea have always had their
ups and downs. During glacial times,
rain froze and stayed on land instead of
running into the sea, so sea levels were
low. But when, like now, we are living
in a milder period (interglacial), ice melts
and sea levels rise. Since the beginning
of the last major thaw, about 18,000 years
ago, sea levels have risen by an incredible
120 m (394 ft). During the next 100 years,
the Earth's surface may warm by 3°C
(5.4°F), due to an enhanced greenhouse
effect, causing sea levels to rise by at least
0.5 m (1 ft 7 in) – enough to affect the
lives of millions of people.

LOST CITY OF ATLANTIS
In about 370 BC, the Greek philosopher
Plato described a civilization called
Atlantis, which sank beneath the
waves because the gods were angry.
In fact, the legend may be based on
the ancient Minoan civilization in
the Mediterranean Sea, which was
probably devastated by volcanoes and
earthquakes in about 1450 BC.

SINKING VENICE
During very high tides in St Mark's
Square, Venice, Italy (*left*), visitors tread
carefully along temporary walkways and
wear rubber boots. The city's leading
attraction is its canals, where boats
replace cars. Venice was built in
medieval times on wooden piles
sunk into the marshy ground. It
is sinking by about 1 cm (0.4 in)
each decade, and its buildings
flood several times a year. At the
same time, the Adriatic Sea, which
flows through Venice, is set to rise
by 2.5 cm (1 in) by 2010.

TROPICAL THREAT
Rising seas threaten small tropical
islands. Many lie only 1–2 m (3–6 ft)
above sea level, and could vanish
beneath the waves within the next
few centuries, if global warming
trends continue. The losses could be
catastrophic. Low-lying island states
such as the Maldives in the Indian
Ocean, are highly populated and
harbour rare and exotic wildlife. In
the Florida Keys, USA (*right*), small
islands are of historical and wildlife
interest. Their disappearence will
threaten the local tourist industry.

BUILDING A SEA WALL

As sea levels rise, low-lying developed countries, such as the Netherlands, are spending huge amounts of money building sea defences. In 1953 a high tide, coupled with a storm surge, overwhelmed the Netherlands' coast. It killed about 1,800 people and destroyed 43,000 homes. The same surge also caused Britain's worst peace-time natural disaster, claiming 300 lives.

PROTEST PRESSURE

At the 1992 Earth Summit in Brazil, environmental groups helped to pressure world leaders into signing the UN Convention on Climate Change. But progress in cutting greenhouse gas emissions has been slow. Developed countries, such as the USA, still produce a large portion of the world's greenhouse gases. Despite this, the developed countries are less likely to be affected by climate change – and rising sea levels – than poor countries in tropical regions. Large areas of Bangladesh are less than 2 m (6 ft) above sea level and millions of people there are affected by floods caused by cyclone surges.

FLORIDA KEYS

Florida's coastline is threatened by erosion, rising sea levels, and storm surges. This map shows what would happen if the sea were to rise by 7.5 m (25 ft). Vast areas of the state would be swamped, including the city of Miami. Such an event is unlikely in the next few hundred years, but even a 1 m (3 ft) sea level rise would cover many of Florida's beaches and endanger wildlife.

ATLANTIC OCEAN

FLORIDA

CAPE CANAVERAL

GULF OF MEXICO

THE EVERGLADES

MIAMI

FLORIDA KEYS

☐ Florida coastline

☐ Florida after flooding

CRUEL SEA

HURRICANES AND TSUNAMIS ARE among the worst catastrophes the oceans can deliver. But the sea has many other life-threatening moods. On most shores, tides rise and fall twice a day – sometimes higher than expected. Their ebb and flow generate strong currents that can stir up great whirlpools in the sea. Tall waves blown up by storms combine to create massive rogue waves that swamp ships. Storm waves strike the shore with immense power, and carve the coastline. Dangers also fall from the sky as a result of twisting waterspouts, while sea fogs can cause ships to collide.

BETWEEN EXTREME TIDES
The gravitational power of the Sun and Moon tugs at the Earth, causing two bulges of sea water to travel around the Earth each day. The bulges produce a high tide with a low tide in between. Twice a month the biggest tides, called spring tides, occur. At this time, the difference between low and high tide can be huge. People may be trapped by rising tides, or caught in tidal currents.

SEA FOG AND MIST
Sea fogs form where warm ocean currents mix with cold. As warm, moist air near the surface of the sea gets cold, its condenses into tiny droplets, creating fog. This happens on the Grand Banks off Newfoundland, Canada, where the cold Labrador Current meets the warm Gulf Stream, which travels from the Gulf of Mexico. Many ships have collided there in poor visibility.

WATERSPOUT
A waterspout is a tornado travelling over water. It looks like a column of water being sucked into the sky, but it is mostly cloudy water vapour. The waterspout's main hazard is the weight of the water it dumps – often several tonnes – when it collapses. It could easily sink a boat

WHIRLPOOLS

A whirlpool is a giant nightmare version of the swirling water that disappears down a plughole. The biggest whirlpools form alongside powerful tidal currents. The Saltstraumen whirlpool that occurs off the coast of Norway is among the most dangerous. Scientists who launch equipment into whirlpools such as the Saltstraumen have seen it sucked down, hit the sea floor, and spat back out!

ROGUE WAVES

In the open sea, storm waves can stack together to form terrifying walls of water called rogue waves. Off Africa's southeast coast, rogue waves form where Southern Ocean storm waves meet the oncoming Agulhas Current. The waves slow and build to become steep and dangerous. Such waves, tens of metres tall, have claimed many vessels.

WAVE ATTACK!

When wind-driven waves reach the shore, they have immense power. A wave 1 m (3 ft) high in shallow water can easily knock you off your feet. A series of pounding 10 m (33 ft) storm waves can cut back chalk cliffs by 1 m (3 ft) overnight. The sea is perpetually eroding and shaping exposed parts of the coast. It unloads its sediment in sheltered water to form beaches.

BURIED TREASURE

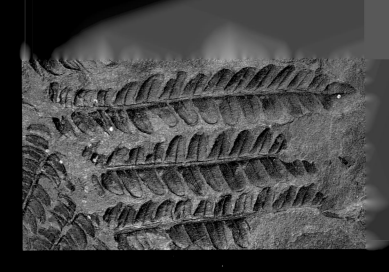

Beneath the Earth's surface is a treasure trove of materials that is constantly being rearranged, sifted, and sorted by geological processes. People have found many uses for these materials, from building roads, to using them as fuel or to decorate jewellery. But it is only when the Earth deposits materials in bulk, and in an accessible place, that they are worth mining. For example, the oceans probably contain about 10 million tonnes of the mineral gold, but it is too thinly spread to be worth extracting. Gold is one of the most treasured of the Earth's many minerals. Unless they can be recycled, the supply of many minerals will eventually become exhausted, as underground reserves are used up.

ANCIENT PLANT ENERGY
During a period 280–345 million years ago, primitive land plants the size of modern trees thrived in vast swamps. When their remains were buried without decaying, heat and pressure gradually converted them to coal, creating many of the coal seams we mine today. Burning coal releases the sunlight energy captured by these ancient plants.

BLACK GOLD
Coal is a valuable fuel. People have been mining it since the Middle Ages. At first, many mines were open-cast, and exposed coal could simply be dug from the land's surface. Nowadays, most coal is mined from seams hundred of metres below ground, although in some places, such as here in southern Chile (*above*), coal is even salvaged from the sea.

FROM PLANKTON TO FUEL
Oil and natural gas are derived from marine plankton that have died and fallen to the sea floor. Over millions of years, as sediment accumulates on top, heat and pressure gradually transform plankton remains into petroleum oil. If the process continues, oil becomes gas. Many oil and gas deposits on land are becoming depleted, so prospectors have turned their attention to deposits beneath the sea floor, for example, in the North Sea (*left*).

GRAVEL PIT

We use sediment deposits dug from the ground to build towns, cities, and roads, and to help grow our food. For example, sand and limestone are used to make concrete, and potash is mined for fertilizer. Many sediment deposits were once beaches and river channels that became buried. They have since been uplifted, or exposed by erosion.

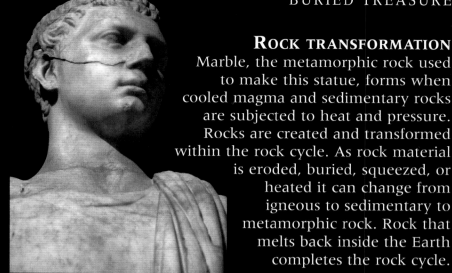

ROCK TRANSFORMATION

Marble, the metamorphic rock used to make this statue, forms when cooled magma and sedimentary rocks are subjected to heat and pressure. Rocks are created and transformed within the rock cycle. As rock material is eroded, buried, squeezed, or heated it can change from igneous to sedimentary to metamorphic rock. Rock that melts back inside the Earth completes the rock cycle.

UNCUT DIAMOND

KOH-I-NOOR DIAMOND

MINE POLLUTION

Some naturally occurring metals are valuable because they are scarce and desirable. Many, such as copper, tin, tungsten, lead, and aluminium, are found in combination with elements within metal-rich ores. Others, such as gold, silver, and platinum, exist on their own as native elements. Mining for metals can cause pollution. Metals leaching from this huge copper mine in Utah, USA (*below*), have made the local ground water unfit to drink.

ROUGH AND SMOOTH

Gems are highly prized crystals. Some – such as topaz – form inside igneous rock. Diamonds emerge from carbon compressed inside metamorphic rock. Most gems, such as sapphires, opals, and rubies, are created by

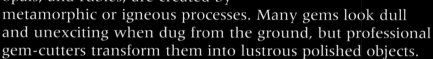

UNCUT TOPAZ

POLISHED TOPAZ

metamorphic or igneous processes. Many gems look dull and unexciting when dug from the ground, but professional gem-cutters transform them into lustrous polished objects.

GLOBAL ECOSYSTEMS

O N LAND, CLIMATE AND SOIL INFLUENCE which plants grow where. In turn, the plants determine which animals thrive locally. In this way, biomes – great global ecosystems – become established. There are about ten biomes. Travelling from the poles to the Equator, biomes change as the climate changes from ice-covered expanses in polar regions to the hot deserts of the tropics. Human activities can change biomes. Temperate grasslands, for example, form naturally in mild climates where there is insufficient water to support the lush growth of trees. But in Europe and North America, thousands of years of tree cutting and animal grazing have replaced many forests with grasslands. Further change has occurred where grassland has been turned into vast fields for cereal crops.

TROPICAL RAINFOREST

Lush, tropical rainforest (*above*) develops where strong sunlight and high rainfall combine with warm temperatures all year round. Various communities of plants and animals live in different layers of the rainforest, from ground level to tree tops. Rainforests contain the greatest diversity of organisms of any biome on land – at least two million species.

SAVANNAH

Savannah develops in tropical areas where rainfall is highly seasonal. Typically, savannahs are grasslands scattered with small trees or shrubs. The savannahs of East Africa are famous for their spectacular big mammals, from giraffes and antelope, to lions and elephants. About 12,000 years ago, large areas of North America supported savannahs containing big cats, elephants, and giant ground sloths. These were hunted to extinction and the landscape has since been tamed for agriculture.

BOREAL FOREST

Boreal forest, or taiga, grows in cold temperate regions of the northern hemisphere. Here, a lack of rainfall and long cool seasons, produce conifers – spruces, pines, and firs – and broadleaved evergreens rather then deciduous trees (those that seasonally shed their leaves). Some boreal forests remain prime targets for extracting softwood timber for furniture and packaging, and pulpwood for making paper. Boreal forests, like tropical rainforests, are recognized as important "lungs of the Earth". They remove atmospheric carbon dioxide and replace it with oxygen.

TUNDRA

Tundra forms in regions of the Arctic where winters are too long and too cold (below -10°C (14°F) for at least half the year) to support the growth of trees. The short, ice-free summers encourage a growth of grasses, mosses, lichens, and dwarf shrubs. During the summer, caribou (reindeer) graze in the area, and migrating birds arrive to nest, and feed upon the vegetation and dense populations of flies and mosquitoes.

TEMPERATE FOREST

Deciduous broadleaved forests are typical of temperate regions, where the climate is humid but winters are cold. Most of the trees stop growing and lose their leaves in winter. Beeches (*right*), oaks, hickories, and maples dominate this woodland, while birch, hazel, and sycamore grow closer to the rich soil. This forest is home to animals such as deer and foxes.

SCRUBLAND

This shrub-covered landscape is found in Mediterranean-type climates, with cool, wet winters, and hot, dry summers. This landscape is called chaparral in North America, mallee in Australia, fynbos in South Africa, and mattoral in Chile. Trees are small, and thorny shrubs and aromatic herb plants predominate. Aromatic oils can spontaneously burst into flame in high summer, starting fires.

ASTEROID STRIKE!

THE GREATEST THREAT TO OUR SURVIVAL may come from space. Our corner of the galaxy is full of chunks of rock and icy debris – asteroids and comets – left over from the birth of the Solar System. You can see them in the night sky as they hurtle through space, falling through our atmosphere and producing shooting stars. Governments are becoming increasingly aware of the danger posed by large, fast-moving objects that could one day collide with the Earth, and are using powerful telescopes to detect them in plenty of time. If a large space rock were on a collision course with our planet, a means might be found to deflect, break it up, or destroy it, perhaps by exploding nuclear warheads nearby. We would have to rely on our technology to save us.

THE TUNGUSKA EVENT
Space rocks do not have to hit the Earth to have a devastating effect. In 1908, there was an explosion 6 km (4 miles) up in the atmosphere, above the unpopulated Tunguska region of Siberia. It was caused by the disintegration of a small asteroid. The blast flattened trees up to 30 km (18 miles) away.

EXTINCTION EVENT
An asteroid 1 km (0.6 miles) wide, striking land or shallow sea, would obliterate everything within 500 km (300 miles). The impact would eject vast amounts of dust into the atmosphere, blocking out most sunlight for a year or more. This would have a catastrophic effect on global climate and agriculture. Scientists estimate there is a one in 10,000 risk of such an Earth-shattering event happening in the 21st century.

BIG AND DANGEROUS

Some 50,000 years ago, a meteorite thought to be 60 m (197 ft) across smashed into northeast Arizona, USA. Hitting the ground at 40,000 kmh (25,000 mph), the solid meteorite vaporized upon impact in a blinding flash and blasted out a crater 1,265 m (1,385 yd) wide (*above*). The explosion would have killed every living thing within 10 km (6 miles).

JUPITER RENDEZVOUS

In March 1993, Jupiter's powerful gravitational field tore comet Shoemaker-Levy-9 into 21 fragments. In July 1994, the fragments collided with Jupiter, producing impact splashes as wide as the Earth. Jupiter's gravity acts as the Solar System's "vacuum cleaner", sucking in many objects that might otherwise strike the Earth.

THE MOON – AN IMPACT RECORD

Impact craters are not that easy to find on Earth. Weathering and erosion have gradually obliterated them. But the Moon, which is geologically inactive and lacks an atmosphere, retains all its scars. Old craters on its surface (*above*) show that impacts were larger and more frequent during the Solar System's early history than they are today.

MEGATSUNAMI

Some 65 million years ago an object 10 km (6 mile) wide struck the Yucatán Peninsula at the edge of the Gulf of Mexico. This was probably the extinction event that wiped out the dinosaurs. Its impact also produced megatsunamis. Vast areas of buried sediment reveal that waves 1 km (0.6 miles) high crashed onto shores of the southern United States and the Caribbean islands.

SAVAGE FUTURE

WHAT DOES THE FUTURE HOLD FOR US? Is a natural disaster looming on the horizon? Or will something created by human actions be our undoing? Major geological hazards affecting millions of people could be unleashed within the next century. The possibilities include a super-volcanic eruption in Yellowstone Park, USA, a landslide in the Canary Islands sending a megatsunami across the Atlantic, and a giant earthquake crippling Tokyo, Japan. But top of the list of near-future hazards are those caused by global warming – sea level rise, flooding, and extreme weather. Where natural disasters are concerned, it pays to plan for the future and to minimize damage to the environment, but expect the unexpected...

COOLER OR WARMER?

Ironically, global warming may also cool the Earth. If polar ice continues to melt, fresh water would gather in the surface waters of polar seas. This would alter the way ocean currents move and may stop warm currents, such as the Gulf Stream, bringing mild weather to northwest Europe, causing it to become much colder.

DRIED UP EARTH

As the Earth warms, some areas, such as parts of California, USA (*above*), will become hotter and drier, making it even harder for life to exist. Extensive over-grazing by animals on the edge of desert areas will lead to increased desertification, as plant cover is reduced and there is less soil to retain water. The destruction of habitats such as these could cause the loss of many plants and animals, altering the balance of nature with unknown effects.

UNDER WATER

The best guess for the next two centuries is that the world will become warmer. Rising temperatures make seawater expand and polar ice melt, raising sea levels by about 1 m (3 ft 3 in) in the next 200 years, devastating low-lying tropical islands and countries. A warming climate is also likely to make weather more extreme, meaning there could be more storms and severe floods, such as this one in Kenya (*right*).

DEFORESTATION

Since 1945, more than 40 per cent of the world's tropical rainforest has been destroyed, and more is being lost every year. Here (*left*), a section of the Amazon rainforest is being cleared. After trees are removed, the fragile topsoil is often washed away so trees cannot regrow. Forests play a vital role in replenishing the atmosphere's oxygen and absorbing carbon dioxide. This important role is threatened because we are removing forest faster than we are replacing it.

OVER-FISHING

Technology today enables fishermen to find and catch entire shoals of fish. By the 1990s, 13 of the world's 17 major fisheries were being fished to the limit or were over-fished. In the early 1990s, Canada restricted access to cod fisheries in the northeast Atlantic because harvesting had dramatically reduced fish populations. In 2001, North Sea cod fishing was also halted. Over-fishing and over-hunting have devastated animal populations. Many will never recover.

STAPHYLOCOCCI
BACTERIA

COMBATING BACTERIA

Disease-causing bacteria, such as staphylococci (*left*) that cause pneumonia and blood poisoning, are becoming resistant to the antibiotics used to control them. Unless medical advances keep ahead, fighting bacterial diseases could return us to the days before antibiotics, when common diseases like tuberculosis (TB) killed millions of people.

GAIA

According to the Gaia hypothesis of British scientist James Lovelock, the Earth and its lifeforms function as if they were a single living organism, regulating their own global climate. This would mean that the Earth naturally changes its environment to maintain the right conditions for life. Even if humans make the Earth unfit for most lifeforms by polluting it and degrading its resources, the Earth would find a way of surviving – without humans if necessary.

EARTH DATA

EARTH RECORDS

Biggest volcanic eruption About 74,000 years ago Mount Toba in Sumatra erupted. The volcano's crater left a hole 100 km (62 miles) long by 60 km (37 miles) wide.

Worst floods In 1931, a 30-m (98-ft) rise in China's Yangtze River caused floods and famine. About 3.5 million people died.

Highest earthquake death toll In 1556, earthquakes in China killed about 800,000 people.

Worst drought Between 1876 and 1879 about 10 million people starved to death during a drought in northern China.

Worst hailstorm In 1888, grapefruit-sized hailstones pummelled the district of Moradabad in India, killing 246.

Worst series of avalanches During World War I, soldiers fighting in the European Alps used explosives to set off avalanches that would engulf enemy troops. At least 40,000 died.

Most severe tornado outbreak The Tri-state Tornado cluster crossed three central US states in March 1925, killing 689 people.

Highest tsunami On 9 July 1958, a landslide generated a tsunami that reached 524 m (1,720 ft)

high in Alaska, USA.

Worst lightning strike In December 1963, lightning struck a jet aircraft over Maryland, USA, killing 81 people.

Worst avalanche and landslide In 1970, a collapse of ice and rock on Peru's Huascarán Mountain killed more than 20,000 people.

Worst cyclone In 1970, a cyclone in the Bay of Bengal killed about 500,000 people in Bangladesh.

Strongest storm winds The northwest Pacific's Typhoon Tip maintained winds of 305 kmh (190 mph) on 12 October, 1979.

EARTH TIMELINE

13 billion years ago Big Bang creates the Universe.

4.6 billion years ago Earth forms.

4.5 billion years ago Earth is hit by Mars-sized body.

4 billion years ago Earth has cooled and Earth's core, mantle, and crust have formed.

3.5 billion years ago Earliest known life forms are preserved in rock.

2.9 billion years ago Earliest photosynthetic microbes appear (they trap sunlight to make food, and release oxygen).

2.5 billion years ago Oxygen levels rise in the atmosphere.

c.2 billion years ago Early supercontinent forms.

700 million years ago Earliest many-celled life forms are preserved in rock.

570 million years ago Early supercontinent breaks up; many-celled marine animals become abundant and diverse.

500 million years ago Early fish are preserved as fossils.

450 million years ago Caledonian mountain-building begins in what will become Scotland, Norway, and the eastern United States.

350 million years ago Tree-like ferns, clubmosses, and horsetails have appeared. Their remains will form major coal deposits. Early reptiles have appeared.

320 million years ago The first flying insects appear.

290 million years ago New supercontinent Pangaea forms.

225 million years ago Supercontinent Pangaea begins to

break up to form Laurasia and Gondwanaland.

140 million years ago Early flowering plants have appeared.

65 million years ago Dinosaurs become extinct probably as a result of a meteorite impact, and the climate change that followed.

55 million years ago Indian subcontinent collides with Asia.

c.3 million years ago Stone tools are being used by human-like beings.

c.2 million years ago Most recent major Ice Age begins.

c.15,000 years ago Current interglacial period begins.

c.1850 Atmospheric carbon dioxide levels begin to rise noticeably as a result of air pollution.

1990s Hottest decade on record.

EARTH FACTS

- The Earth averages a distance of 149,600,000 km (92,960,000 miles) from the Sun.
- The Earth is not exactly round, but bulges slightly at the Equator, where it measures 40,024 km (24,870 miles) around. The diameter of the Earth is 12,715 km (7,900 miles) at the Poles, and 43 km (27 miles) more than this at the Equator.
- The temperature at the centre of the Earth is believed to be about 5,000°C (9,000°F) and the pressure about 3.5 million atmospheres.
- The Earth weighs about 5,976 billion billion tonnes (6,574 billion billion US tons).

EARTHQUAKE CATEGORIES

Mercalli scale	Description	Effects	Richter scale
I	Instrumental	Recorded by instruments but not felt.	Less than 4.3
II	Feeble	Felt by people on upper floors.	
III	Minor	Indoors, feels like a heavy truck passing by; hanging objects swing.	
IV	Moderate	Outdoors, felt by walkers; indoors, crockery rattles.	4.3–4.8
V	Slightly strong	Sleepers awake; doors swing.	
VI	Strong	Windows break; hanging pictures fall; walking difficult.	4.8–6.1
VII	Very strong	Plaster and tiles fall; standing difficult large church bells ring.	
VIII	Destructive	Chimneys fall; car steering affected.	6.1–6.9
IX	Ruinous	General panic; some buildings collapse.	
X	Disastrous	Many buildings destroyed.	6.9–7.3
XI	Very disastrous	Most buildings and bridges collapse; railway tracks bend; roads break up.	7.3–8.1
XII	Catastrophic	Total destruction; ground waves seen; vision distorted.	8.1–8.9

VOLCANIC EXPLOSIVITY INDEX (VEI)

Volcanic explosivity index (VEI)	Description	Height of eruption column km (miles)	Eruption rate tonnes/ second
0	Effusive	Below 0.1 (0.06)	0.1–1
1	Gentle	0.1–1 (0.06–0.6)	1–10
2	Explosive	1–5 (0.6–3)	10–100
3	Severe	3–15 (2–9)	100–1,000
4	Violent	10–25 (6–15)	1,000-10,000
5	Cataclysmic	25+ (15+)	10,000–100,000
6	Paroxysmal	25+ (15+)	100,000–1,000,000
7	Colossal	25+ (15+)	1,000,000–10,000,000
8	Terrific	25+ (15+)	More than 10,000,000

GLOSSARY

Abyssal plain Broad, flat expanse at the bottom of an ocean basin.

Acid rain Rain made more acidic by some types of air pollution.

Asteroid Small body of rock, orbiting the Sun, left over from the birth of the Solar System.

Atmosphere Gas-rich layer surrounding the Earth.

Atoll Ring of coral that forms on the site of a sunken volcanic island.

Black smoker Chimney of deposits on the sea floor through which a black jet of superheated, chemical-rich water gushes.

Chalk Soft limestone made up mostly of the skeletons of dead, microscopic algae called coccolithophorids.

Clay Sediment composed of very fine particles of weathered rock.

Climate Weather conditions in a particular area averaged over 30 years or more.

Comet A mass of ice and rock hurtling through near Space. Sunlight melts some of the ice, producing a comet's tail.

Core Dense, hot iron-rich centre of the Earth

Crust Outer rocky layer of the Earth, varying between 5 – 80 km (3 – 50 miles) in thickness.

Earthquake Shaking of the Earth's crust caused when tectonic plates slide past or over each other.

Epicentre The place on Earth's surface that lies directly above the focus of an earthquake.

Erosion The processes by which rock or soil are loosened and transported by agents such as glaciers, rivers, wind and waves.

Fault Fracture in Earth's crust where one rock slides past another.

Focus Point below the Earth's surface from which an earthquake's shock waves originate.

Fossils Remains or traces of living things preserved in Earth's rocks.

Geologist Scientist who studies the Earth's surface and rocks, and the processes by which they are created, transformed and broken down.

Glacier Mass of ice and snow flowing slowly downhill under its own weight.

Global warming Gradual increase in the average temperature across the world.

Greenhouse effect The trapping of infrared radiation from the Earth's surface by greenhouse gases in the atmosphere, producing a warming effect.

Guyot Volcanic island that has eroded and subsided beneath the waves, producing a flat-topped, underwater feature.

Hot spot Place in the Earth's mantle, well away from a plate boundary, where hot rock burns through the crust, creating volcanoes.

Ice Age Cold period during Earth's geological history. During an Ice Age there are very cold periods (glacial maxima) when ice sheets and glaciers advance, and warmer periods (interglacials) when they retreat.

Igneous rock Rock formed by molten rock from the Earth's interior cooling and solidifying on the surface or underground.

Lava Hot, molten rock that emerges from volcanoes.

Limestone Sedimentary rock composed mainly of calcium carbonate (calcite).

Magma Hot, molten rock below Earth's surface.

Mantle The deep layer of rock – part solid, part molten – that lies underneath Earth's crust.

Meteorite Rock, falling from space, that strikes the Earth.

Metamorphic rock Rock formed by the alteration of existing solid rock by heat or pressure.

Mid-ocean ridge Zig-zagging ridge on the sea floor at the boundary where two plates move apart.

Mineral Naturally occurring chemical – either a single element or a combination of elements – found within rock.

Moraine Debris deposited by a glacier, especially sand and gravel.

Ozone layer Gas layer, derived from the element oxygen, that forms high in Earth's atmosphere. It provides some protection against the Sun's ultraviolet radiation.

Pangaea Supercontinent which existed 225 million years ago, and broke apart, becoming the continents that exist today.

Planet A large mass that orbits a star. In our Solar System, nine planets, including the Earth, orbit the Sun.

Plate tectonics Movement of Earth's tectonic plates.

Rock Large, solid mass exposed at Earth's surface and composed of one or more minerals.

Rock cycle Cycle summarizing the creation and transformation of rocks (igneous, metamorphic, and sedimentary).

Sediment Debris loosened and transported by weathering and erosion, and deposited elsewhere.

Sedimentary rock Rock formed from sediment.

Seismometer (seismograph) Instrument that detects and records vibrations in the ground such as those produced by an earthquake's shock waves.

Solar System The Sun and the bodies that orbit it, including planets, moons, and asteroids.

Stalactite A hanging, icicle-like structure composed largely of calcium carbonate (calcite).

Stalagmite A rising, candle-like structure composed largely of calcium carbonate (calcite).

Strata Layers of sedimentary rock.

Subduction One tectonic plate descending below another.

Tectonic plate One of 20 or so giant slabs of rock that form the Earth's crust. They move slowly across Earth's surface.

Trench A deep depression in the sea floor where one tectonic plate is forced down below another.

Tsunami Large sea wave that travels across the ocean following an earthquake, volcanic eruption, or impact by a large mass.

Volcano Opening in Earth's crust from which lava escapes.

Weather Day-to-day atmospheric conditions affecting a particular locality.

Weathering Physical, chemical, or biological breakdown of rocks on Earth's surface.

EARTH WEBSITES

www.bghrc.com
Cutting-edge natural disaster research courtesy of Benfield Greig Hazard Research Centre.

www.dsc.discovery.com/guides/planetearth/planetearth.html
Discovery Channel's planet Earth site.

www.crustal.ucsb.edu/ics/understanding/
Understanding Earthquakes educational site.

http://earthquake.usgs.gov/
USGS Earthquake Hazards Program will have you quaking in your shoes.

www.geophys.washington.edu/tsunami/welcome.html
Tsunami ahoy!

http://volcano.und.nodak.edu/
Catch up on the latest volcanic rumblings at Volcano World.

BACKGROUND SHOWS AMMONITE FOSSILS

INDEX

ACKNOWLEDGMENTS

Dorling Kindersley would like to thank the following people for their help with this book: Kate Bradshaw for editorial assistance; Dawn Davies-Cook, Lisa Lanzarini, Carole Oliver, Robert Perry, and Joanna Pocock for design help; Chris Bernstein for the index.

Additional photography and illustration by Max Alexander, Luciano Corbella, Mike Dunning, Frank Greenaway, Colin Keates, John Lepine, Colin Rose, Colin Salmon, James Stevenson, Matthew Ward, Richard Ward, and Francesca York.

Dorling Kindersley would also like to thank the following for their kind permission to reproduce their photographs:

c=centre; l=left; r=right; b=bottom; t=top

AKG London: 31bl. **Chris Bonington Picture Library:** Doug Scott 17br. **Bruce Coleman Ltd:** 50-51; Astrofoto 4bl, 5cr; Atlantide Snc 45bl; Davis Hughes 38-39; Derek Croucher 29tl; Granville Harris 29c; Hans Reinhard 33bl; Jules Cowan 28-29, 43cr. **Colorific!:** Philippe Hays 51tl. **Corbis:** 9c, 23c, 23t; Annie Griffiths Belt 30-31; Charles Mauzy 32cr; Charles O'Rear 2tl, 20cl; Craig Lovell 20r; Dan Guravich 32br; Dave G. Houser 55tr; David Muench 29crb, 30br; Eric and David Hosking 31tr; Eye Ubiquitous 42tr; Galen Rowell 60cl; Gary Braasch 13t; Gunter Marx Photography 42cl; Historical Picture Archive 23b; Jeremy Horner 38cl; Jim Sugar 52-53; Lowell Georgia 52ca; Marc Muench 7bc; Michael S. Yamashita 11t, 48crb; Owen Franken 21br; PH3 James Collins 53cr; Philip J. Corwin 13bl; Ralph White 24tr, 27tl; Robert Estall 52cl; Roger

Ressmeyer 10cl, 11cr, 13cr, 14cl; Stephanie Maze 44bl; Tom Bean 34-35; Wild Country 16-17. **Environmental Images:** Steve Morgan 45tr. **Robert Harding Picture Library:** 36bc; Dr. A. C. Waltham 37br; E. Simanor 39br; Gavin Hellier 34bc; Gene Moore 47br; Nigel Gomm 30cl; Simon Harris 39tr; Tomlinson 11bl. **Hutchison Library:** A. Eames 17tr; Robert Francis 12. **The Image Bank:** Joseph Devenney 52bl. **Images Colour Library:** 22-23. **FLPA - Images of nature:** S. Jonasson 25t. **Museo Archeologico Nazionale di Napoli:** 13cl. **NASA:** 61br. **Natural History Museum:** 44c. **N.H.P.A.:** A. N/ T. 40cl; Alberto Nardi 57bl; B. Jones & M. Shimlock 45bl; Daniel Heuclin 54tr; David Woodfall 51tr; Laurie Campbell 25bl; R. Sorensen & J. Olsen 57c; Rod Planck 39bl; Trevor McDonald 54bl. **NOAA / National Geophysical Data Center:** 24cl. **Oxford Scientific Films:** Alan Root 41bc; Andrea Ghisotti 6br; Caroline Brett 41br; Colin Monteath 34cl; David B. Fleetham 15c; Doug Allan 1, 40-41; Kent Wood 47t;

Kynan Bazley/Hedgehog House 36-37; NASA 24br; Warren Faidley 46b. **PA Photos:** EPA European Press Agency 18-19, 19tr. **Chris and Helen Pellant:** 17cl. **Rex Features:** 31br, 36c, 40bc, 47cr, 47bl, 49; M. Leon/Medianews 37cr; Niko/Coret/Sipa Press 36cl; Oshihara 21t. **San Francisco Public Library:** 20bl. **Science Museum:** 21bl. **Science Photo Library:** A. Gragera, Latin Stock 58bl; Andrew Syred 27br; Bernhard Edmaier 14-15, 14b, 35tl; Celestial Image Co. 5tc; David Hardy 50tc; David Nunuk 39c; David Parker 9t, 18t; Doug Allan 33t; Dr. Karl Lounatmaa 61bl; Dr. Morley Read 56tr, 61tl; Dr. Peter Moore 35tr; George Holton 43tl; Institute of Oceanographic Sciences/NERC 26tr; J. G. Galdzer 52br; J. G. Paren 33br; JISAS 7tr; Juergen Berger, Max-Planck Institute 27cr; Julian Baum 8br; Martin Land 8br; Mehau Kulyk 4-5; MSSSO, ANU 59cb; NASA 5br, 10br, 44-45, 59cl, 59br; NOAA 41tc, 43tr; Novosti Press Agency 58tr; Pekka Par;ainen 6tr; Pekka Perviainen 59t;

Peter Menzel 2-3, 42-43; Simon Fraser 9bl, 28bl, 32bl, 57br; Sinclair Stammers 28cl, 62-63; Tom McHugh 60tr; UK Meteorological Office 45tl; William Ervin 56bc. **Frank Spooner Pictures:** Kaku Kurita 3tc, 15cl. **Still Pictures:** Adrian Arbib 50bl; Daniel Dancer 55b; DERA 46cr; G. Griffiths - Christian Aid 48-49c, 60br; Julio Etchart/Reportage 54cr; Mark Edwards 55tl, 61cr; Patrick Bertrand 57tl; Roland Seitre 56bl. **Getty Images:** Paul Chesley 19tl. **Woods Hole Oceanographic Institution:** 27cl. **Woodfall Wild Images:** David Woodfall 48cl

Jacket Credits:

Getty Images: Schafer and Hill front; **Oxford Scientific Films:** Doug Allan inside front; **Corbis:** Charles O'Rear back cbr, Roger Ressmeyer back clb and inside back; **PA Photos:** European Press Agency back cbl; **Rex Features:** back crb.